Kayak Fly Fishing

EVERYTHING YOU NEED TO KNOW TO START CATCHING FISH

Ben Duchesney

STACKPOLE
BOOKS

Guilford, Connecticut

Published by Stackpole Books
An imprint of Globe Pequot
Trade Division of The Rowman & Littlefield Publishing Group, Inc.
4501 Forbes Boulevard, Suite 200, Lanham, Maryland 20706

Distributed by NATIONAL BOOK NETWORK
800-462-6420

Photos by Ben Duchesney unless otherwise credited

British Library Cataloguing in Publication Information available

Library of Congress Cataloging-in-Publication Data available

ISBN 978-0-8117-1768-7 (paperback)
ISBN 978-0-8117-6605-0 (e-book)

∞™ The paper used in this publication meets the minimum requirements of American National Standard for Information Sciences—Permanence of Paper for Printed Library Materials, ANSI/NISO Z39.48-1992.

Printed in the United States of America

Contents

Part 2: Hitting the Water 91

Acknowledgments

I couldn't have done this without you, Jennie. Also, a huge thanks to all of those who helped with this book, including the many anglers who were kind enough to share their secrets with me and the book's readers.

Hansom
TACKLE

Introduction

One time in a tackle shop, a friend mentioned out loud that I fly fish from a kayak. Behind the counter, the tackle shop worker's eyes widened and he asked, "Do you do it upside down, too? That might be easier."

It may look like some sort of voodoo black magic to some, standing in a kayak and fly casting, but with modern kayak designs, fast rods, and a halfway decent sense of balance, it's an easily attainable goal. I tell people all the time that they should at least give fly fishing from a kayak a chance. Once you tailor your techniques of casting and paddling a certain way, to better suit your fishing platform, you can easily take advantage of this super-stealthy form of fishing. I spend most of my time, besides behind a desk, out on the saltwater flats of Cape Cod, Massachusetts, standing in my kayak as the 12-foot tides race by, looking for signs of striped bass. Sure, I occasionally fish from a big center console, or even wade, but given the choice, I'll always choose the kayak.

I didn't always fish this way. In fact, I only started fly fishing in college after borrowing a fly rod from my little brother and half-sliding, half-falling down the side of a mountain to reach a trout steam behind the school. Spending every minute before, after, and between class (and sometimes instead of), I fell in love with the simplicity of the cast, the poetry in the motions, and, of course, the beautiful fish.

Author Ben Duchesney scans the waters surrounding a sandbar in the middle of the flats of Cape Cod, looking for striped bass on the fly. This is the exact sandbar where he fell in love with kayak fly fishing.

Shortly before I picked up a fly rod, I picked up a paddle. Spending plenty of time in different boats as a kid growing up in a coastal town, having my own craft was always a dream. I thought it was a very distant dream until I graduated high school and was gifted my first kayak. The first generation of fishing kayaks were just hitting the stores, and I was blessed with a kayak that wasn't a dog to paddle, allowed me to stand in it all day long without falling into the drink, and had enough storage space to fit my tackle gear.

I spent the following winter and many of the following seasons rigging and re-rigging and perfecting the layout of my first kayak until it was an absolute fishing machine. Constantly tweaking and improving your boat's performance is another major joy of kayak fly fishing. Not only can you keep improving your boat and your gear, but more importantly, you will forever be learning. Never again can you call yourself an expert on fishing or paddling because once you do, you've closed yourself off to learning another great new paddle stroke or cast that will surely help you.

When I first started kayak fishing, I never considered it paddling, or myself a paddler. It wasn't until I started spending time on the water with real paddlers did I see the magic that lies within the proper technique and a high level of skill. Instead of muscling my way through a wave or fighting the current of a river or the tide, I quickly learned to harness that energy. Instead of wearing myself out, getting frustrated while paddling, I was putting more time and effort into fishing and enjoying paddling the whole time. The further along you get with your paddling skills, the more your fishing will benefit. To the same effect, the better your skill becomes at fly casting, especially with the subtle nuances of casting from a kayak, the more you'll enjoy paddling and kayaking.

There are many microskiffs and other lightweight boats that are designed to get into the skinniest water and be almost imperceptible to the fish. Sure, these boats come close to what I can do in a kayak, but I'm able to go places that even they can only dream of. I've been deeper and farther into the backwaters of a fishery in a kayak than I'd ever be able to with any other vessel and cast to fish that think they're safe.

Fly fishing adds to that stealth factor by allowing me to present flies in super-skinny water, or throw patterns and flies that are so subtle in their presentation that the fish can't help but bite. Whether it's in fast-moving rivers or big expansive flats, in a backwoods wilderness lake or your local bass pond, a fly rod and a kayak can be two of the deadliest tools that will get you on more fish.

When I was the web editor of *Kayak Angler* magazine, I got to travel all over the country, even up into Canada, to go fishing. No matter where I go, whether I get to bring my own gear or not, I always try to throw a fly if I get the chance. Doesn't matter the species. I've begged fishing guides to bring along an extra fly rod, strapped a travel rod onto the back of a motorcycle, and even decided to leave the conventional or spinning gear at home if it means I can throw a fly. If I'm sitting or standing comfortably on a kayak, my fly is the

Ben Duchesney sifts through his fly box for a bushy, hairy streamer that will fool a big smallmouth bass on Cape Cod. Once you start fly fishing from a kayak, your life is going to be changed forever.

one that hooks into a fish, even when no one else can connect.

Another thing about kayak fly fishing is that it's just damn fun. Whether or not I'm the only one catching fish, which more often than not isn't the case, I know that I'm having more fun throwing a fly in a kayak than I would be fishing from a different boat or with different gear. The soft pull of water on my paddle drifting into a quiet freshwater cove, the zing of line through my guides when I shoot it towards a tailing fish, surfing waves on the paddle home—it all adds up to a richer experience.

Another big difference that really separates this form of fishing from any other kind is that this is real work and real exercise. Instead of sitting in a swiveling chair at the front of a boat, powered by big twin motors that require you to only push a button or two, you're your own motor. Every ounce of sweat and effort that you put into kayak fly fishing is returned twofold. Any time I feel I'm slacking off on the water is a day where I haven't seen many fish and likely haven't paddled very far from shore. The anglers who are emboldened by determination when they try this artful pursuit are the anglers who will reap the rewards of a lifetime of passion and adventure.

Instead of smelling gas or wondering if my motor's batteries are running low, or being nervous about my big boat or engines scaring off the fish and every other creature for miles, I can paddle silently along and listen. Instead of blasting my eardrums with wind-noise, the wind rustles through the leaves overhead or rolls across the flats into a warm blanket of salty air.

Even if everyone else is catching fish while I'm getting skunked, I'm still having more fun because I get to enjoy casting, rather than wearing my arms out by throwing some heavy lure, cast after cast after cast. Which is another joy of fly fishing from a kayak. If you can't catch fish, which happens to the best of us, you still get to enjoy a nice paddle, rather than think about the money you just burned in your gas tank.

Whether you're fishing pressured bass ponds, eddy-hopping on backwater creeks or rivers for trout, looking for a wall hanger of a musky, or stalking the saltwater flats for a giant in skinny water, fly fishing from a kayak gives you the best odds. Use a fly rod and kayak together and switch to stealth mode the next time you go out fishing.

Once you have combined these two art forms, these great passions, you'll have a life full of learning and progressing, constantly getting better at one or the other, which then helps both. Instead of fighting the forces seemingly against you, you'll be able to harness that energy and drive it into the proper paddle stroke or know the necessary cast to make it work for you.

Just be careful—once you start fly fishing from a kayak and take this path, there's really no turning back.

PART 1

Getting Started

OCEAN KAYAK

CHAPTER 1

Choosing the Right Boat

I have an addiction to boats. I'll admit it. It's probably so far along, so deeply rooted in my psyche, that not admitting it would be useless. So much so that admitting it is almost a part of the addiction. Like I'm proud of the obsession. Maybe I am.

I currently have so many boats in my possession that I could run a paddling school with every kind of craft imaginable. Of course, I have multiple fishing kayaks. Some are perfect for cruising the saltwater flats, while others I save for freshwater excursions. Some I use any time I'm in moving water, and some I use just when I don't feel like carrying or dragging anything heavy. Some I don't even use—I just let others borrow them so I can fish with more friends. See, there's nothing wrong with too many fishing kayaks.

I also have a canoe, a whitewater creek boat, and the ability to use a friend's center console whenever I want, so therefore it's mine. I have an inflatable drift boat that's perfect for those long days on the water with a buddy. I even have a few recreational sit-inside kayaks for general horseplay and kayaking when I don't plan on wetting a line—though I usually still bring along a rod because, well, why *wouldn't* I bring one?

The point is, once you pick the right boat for your needs, something that will grow with you as you learn and progress in your skills, you'll fall in love with paddling even more. When I first started paddling, my kayak didn't paddle like a barge, but it certainly wasn't sleek and speedy. Once I started

Fly fishing from a kayak means you can fish any water you find, from small kettle ponds like this for smallmouth bass to the open ocean. There's a kayak for you out there, it just depends on how you want to fish.

Putting in at low tide to fish for skinny-water striped bass on the flats of Cape Cod means a long drag through the mud. Use Google Maps to find the closest access point to reach the fishery without hiking or dragging your boat too far.

experimenting and cheating on that boat with others, I was hooked and started to paddle with any boat I could get my greedy hands on.

With each progression in skill, your love for boats will get deeper and deeper. Your first smooth eddy turn, with the canoe's gunwales almost kissing the water's surface; your first successful surf launch, with your bow crashing through incoming wave after wave, heading out for a long day of kayak fishing; or your first time still standing after a water-skier's wake makes the boat rock like a buoy—each milestone is something that you'll remember, and each boat will leave its mark.

My first boat has come and gone, but I still remember it and all of the fun that we had. As I say hello to new boats and good-bye to old ones, my needs are constantly changing with each new skill I've gained. When I can balance in a super-skinny boat with ease and don't need a craft that is as stable as the ground, I can trade that boat in for a faster one. When I start bringing more or less gear with me on each trip, I can get a boat with the capacity that better suits my needs.

Because kayaks are so much cheaper than bass boats or big motorboats, it's easy to buy, sell, or swap with your buddies and get a boat that exactly matches your needs one day and another boat to exactly match your needs the next.

Am I saying that you need a different boat for every fishery, for every type of fish you're after, or for every emotion you may possibly have during the day? No, that's ridiculous. One day you may find yourself in exactly that position, with so many boats that you don't know how they all found themselves in your shed, but it's not necessary in order to love kayak fly fishing.

Instead of focusing on what boat you want, first start by figuring out exactly what you need. Once you've realized the types of fish you want to catch, the fishery or handful of fisheries that you want to fish, and your fishing style and skill level, you can start to address which boat is exactly right for you.

Often I see a group of friends with the same brand of boat, or even the exact same model. That's fine if you're all fishing the same kinds

A layer of sand on the roof of a car reflects the rising sun at the start of a successful morning fishing for striped bass on Cape Cod. The saltwater flats are where the author feels most at home.

of environments, for the same fish, and you all have the same skill level and style and feel comfortable paddling the same boat as everyone else in your group (just get a different color). But, if your needs aren't exactly the same as your buddies', don't get the same boat.

Start broad and work your way down to the finer points. Start by figuring out where you want to fish and what fish you'll be targeting, then determine your fishing style and skill level. Once you know these things, you can decide which boat fits your needs. Then you can worry about color and other fun things like rigging options, different paddles and gear, and more. Oh, the possibilities!

Sit-Insides vs. Sit-on-Tops

By far the biggest debate in kayak fishing is the battle between sit-inside kayaks and sit-on-tops. A quick glance at any kayak fishing blog or website, especially on social media, would lead the casual observer to believe that the sit-on-top (SOT) is creaming the sit-inside kayak (SINK) in popularity. Don't let this facade fool you. The number of sit-insides that are being used in fishing is likely equal to the number of SOTs. As a general rule, sit-on-tops are used more often by kayak fishing pros, the ones on the factory teams that are all over the pages of magazines and social media. Sit-inside anglers, however, are usually either beginners, as most sit-insides are less expensive, or are highly specialized anglers, like those in very cold climates or fast-moving rivers. These anglers are less likely to be in the spotlight, and therefore many believe sit-on-tops are the only way to fish. But they'd be wrong.

Which boat is right for you depends on your personal needs, where you fish, how you fish, and, of course, your personal preference. While sit-on-tops are great boats for some applications and sit-insides are perfectly suited for others, either boat can excel where you like to fish.

More often than not, the right boat for the right situation depends on hull design and the proper balance of primary and secondary stability. Primary stability is the amount you can lean the boat from one side or the other without going on edge. Secondary stability is the amount of effort it takes for the boat to completely flip over once it has come up on edge. The easiest way to think about primary and secondary stability is to envision a jon boat. A jon boat has very strong primary stability, as in it's difficult for you to tip the boat over because it is so stable. When it comes to secondary stability, though, a jon boat is seriously lacking, which means that if you do manage to tip the boat to one side and push it past its primary stability, you're going over.

On the other hand, a sea kayak—long, skinny, and fast—has a mixture of primary and secondary stability, depending on hull design. A sea kayak usually has a strong enough stability for you to paddle straight all day without falling over, but it can be easily pushed past its primary stability with a slight tilt of your hips, therefore putting it on edge. Usually the secondary stability of a sea kayak

Professional fly tier and Jackson Kayak pro staffer Pat Cohen loads some pre-rigged fly rods into his Kilroy, a sit-inside kayak hybrid that allows him to store gear and shelter himself from harsh conditions at the same time.

is stronger than its primary, meaning you can easily put the boat on edge for easier turning, but it takes a further tilt in order for the boat to fully flip, causing you to then complete a roll in order to right yourself. For kayak fly fishing, however, we usually aren't rolling our kayaks, so a primary stability that is strong enough to instill confidence paired with a strong secondary stability so you won't flip while casting and fishing is the best balance of the two, creating the perfect stability for a fishing kayak.

Should you flip, it is much harder to get back into a sit-inside kayak than it is to get back on top of your sit-on-top. If you flip in your sit-inside, you'll need to perform a self-rescue, or hope that your fishing buddies know how to perform an assisted rescue. It is much easier to assist or be assisted in the event of a capsize, so always try to fish with a buddy. Once you get back into your kayak, you'll likely require a bilge pump to remove any water that has found its way inside your boat. These are inexpensive to buy and don't take up much room inside your kayak, and they can be found at most marine stores or paddling shops.

If you happen to flip your sit-on-top kayak, it is much easier to right your boat and then climb back aboard. Wearing a PFD, or personal flotation device, will help you get back into your boat and keep you much safer on the water. Because sit-on-top kayaks are self-draining, meaning there are holes, called scupper holes, along the entire hull that allow water to pass through and drain the boat, there won't be any water to remove. Make sure to keep all of your hatches closed while fishing and all of your gear tied down—that way water won't get inside your kayak's hull and you won't lose any gear in the drink.

Ponds and Lakes

Deciding which style of boat you need depends on where you like to fish, how you like to fish, how far you need to walk to get to the water, if there is current to think about, and so many other variables that you could sit and argue with yourself at the paddle shop for days. The easiest place to start is to identify what kind of fishery you'll be spending most of your time in. Although there's a good chance you'll be spending time in a variety of situations, since kayak fly fishing can adapt itself so well to many different fisheries, decide where you're most likely to spend the most amount of time.

For anglers that spend a lot of time on small backwoods ponds, I always suggest a simple, lightweight sit-inside kayak. Although a sit-on-top may work just as well if you have a way to get your boat to the water, these anglers most likely will have to hike in on a tight trail, or no trail at all, and a lighter boat will save time, effort, and an endless amount of frustration.

When deciding on the right sit-inside for a small pond in the woods, think about the trail first. A boat that has a wide cockpit will allow you to place the gunwale, or side of the boat, on your shoulder. Many sit-inside kayaks now have padding along the gunwale for exactly this purpose, but you can also add more padding later if you decide you need a little more cushion.

Once you get to the water, you're going to want a boat that is stable enough for your ability. Although it's great to research a boat online, there's nothing like getting your hands on one in a store and really giving it a proper look, flipping the boat over and looking at the hull's design. You'll want to notice a keel line running down the center of the boat, nothing overly pronounced or sharp, but enough to be apparent. That way, when you're paddling straight, you'll have a boat that tracks well, or continues to go straight ahead, without the bow constantly turning from side to side.

Harry Duchesney throws out a long roll cast in the fading light in hopes of fooling a big rainbow trout with an olive Woolly Bugger. Sit-on-top kayaks allow you to stand up for hours on end and cast flies at the same time, with ease.

A kayak cart makes getting your kayak to the water much easier on your boat and your body. Avoid dragging your kayak through gravel or over concrete to prevent damaging it.

MUSTANG

The next feature to look for is a hull shape that will aid in stability. The most stable hull design you'll see is a catamaran-style hull, with the keel almost recessed in the hull so there is space in the center and two round halves of the hull creating two pontoon-like supports. A boat that allows the water to support the boat in multiple places is best, with a hull design that is staged—that way the primary stability and secondary stability will be comfortable for all-day fishing and you won't be paranoid about tipping.

When it comes to a lightweight boat that you can throw over your shoulder, stay away from rotomolded hulls, unless you've been working out. A rotomolded boat is manufactured by pouring plastic inside a mold and then spinning, shaking, and heating the form so that all of the plastic is shaped into a hull. These boats are heavy, as they use more plastic. Thermoforming, on the other hand, creates a lighter boat that you can throw over your shoulder for a long hike to the water. Thermoformed boats are manufactured by placing a sheet of plastic over a heated mold, thus creating a thinner hull that uses less plastic, which results in a lighter boat.

When inspecting the deck, or top, of your pond-hopping sit-inside, look for flat areas that will allow you to install mounts later on for rod holders or other accessories like electronics. Many companies now offer angler versions of their boats that already come with mounting options or rod holders. At the very least, bungees stretched across the deck of the kayak will allow you to quickly stash gear beneath them.

Because these backwater ponds are smaller and you don't need to worry about paddling long distances, a shorter, wider boat will give you the best balance of stability and speed. As a general rule, the longer and skinnier a boat is, the faster it will be, and the wider a boat is, the more stability it will have. Test out different boats before you buy; many paddling shops have demo days on a regular basis that allow you to test as many boats as you like on a local lake. A good pond-hopping boat could be 10 feet long and as wide as 36 inches. A wide, short kayak such as this will give you the strongest stability at a length that will still allow you to put some speed behind your paddle strokes, should you need to make a crossing in the wind or just get back to the trailhead before dark.

For bigger lakes and ponds, where you don't need to worry about hiking in or carrying your boat a long distance, a rotomolded sit-on-top can give you the best options for carrying gear and rigging rod holders or electronics. The latest fishing kayaks have so many rigging options for the kayak fly fisher that some boats look as fancy and rigged up as professional bass boats. For medium-size water, a lake that would take a full day or more to fish, a 12-foot boat would be long enough to get you around fast enough. For bigger lakes, fisheries that would take weeks to completely cover, a boat the size of a sea kayak, around 16 feet long, provides the perfect speed to get you to the fish.

Since you'll be spending more time paddling and less time turning, you'll want a stronger keel—a boat that will track straight

Joe Gugino winds up for a big roll cast in search of Atlantic salmon on the North Shore of Massachusetts. Being able to cast while sitting down is an essential first step to learning how to fly fish from a kayak.

even in heavy winds. The stronger the keel line, the harder it is for a boat to turn, which is why river boats are generally round-bottomed, with no keel at all. On a big lake where distance is a factor, however, you'll spend more time paddling straight than you will turning.

Look for a boat that is as wide as you can stand, but will still allow you to pick up paddling speed for the longer crossings. A sit-on-top that is around 32 to 34 inches wide should have enough stability for you to stand up and cast all day, but still be slicey in the water when you need to put the spurs to your boat and cover some distance. Again, a hull that stages out or that features a catamaran-style design will give you the most stability for standup fishing. When the wind kicks up or you need to cut through chop on long paddle runs, a boat that has enough bow flare, with the sides of the hull flaring out at the front, will deflect oncoming waves away from the boat instead of allowing them to crash over the bow and onto you or your gear.

The top deck of your lake fishing boat should be open enough that you can stand comfortably, without hatches or rigging getting in the way of your feet or line, but have enough flat, empty surfaces to give you versatile mounting platforms. Often a bigger lake will require electronics in order to fully research it and optimize your fishing time. A rear tankwell, the big space behind the seat, allows you to store things like a tackle bag or crate with all of your gear and is also a perfect spot to put a cooler or dry bag.

Many sit-on-tops also feature hatches that allow you to store gear—or fish, should you choose to keep your catch, though I always urge catch-and-release—directly inside the hull itself. This is a perfect spot to store an extra paddle, should you break your primary one, or extra rods, or other nonessential gear that you don't plan on accessing throughout the day, as it can be harder to access these hatches. Day hatches, usually smaller and much closer to the seat, allow you to keep smaller essentials like water, keys, or your wallet handy but out of the way while you're fishing.

Although many new fishing kayaks have very cool camo color schemes or a lot of dark patterns available, for bigger lakes with more boat traffic it's smart to buy a boat that will be highly visible, even at dawn or dusk when you're likely to be on the water but less likely to be noticed. Many manufacturers also offer color schemes, like a bright yellow, that will allow you to be seen by the many pleasure boaters or jet skiers that you're sure to run into on larger, more popular lakes. High-vis clothing or reflective tape is another smart idea. The tape is inexpensive and readily available at most hardware stores, takes seconds to install on your kayak, and will keep you much safer. As always, no matter what body of water you're fishing in, but even more important when fishing in a high-traffic area, wear your PFD so that if you do get flipped by a boat wake or flip in heavy winds, you'll be able to quickly get back onto your kayak and make it to shore.

Rivers

River anglers all have different styles depending on the exact river that they fish, as every river has its unique personality and features, so therefore choosing the right boat for your local river is like choosing a soul mate. You'll never really know which boat is best until you've tried out a few and broken a few hearts, but then the right one will come along and you'll be as smitten as a schoolboy.

The style of boat will usually depend on the river's flow. The faster the current, the more nimble and specialized a boat must be in order to compensate. A slower river can be more like a moving pond and doesn't command a particular style of boat. The right boat style also depends on how you choose to fish a river. Some anglers like to do all of their fishing from their kayak, letting their drift dictate the time spent on every spot, while other

Professional fly tier and Jackson Kayak pro staffer Pat Cohen searches for a cruising Vermont musky with a fly of his own creation, the ManBearPig. The slow river current allows Cohen to work the big, bushy fly more thoroughly, covering more water.

anglers prefer to get out and wade where they can, trailering their kayak behind them on a leash or tether.

Think about how you want to fish the rivers where you'll be spending most of your time. It's harder to get out of a sit-inside kayak than it is to slide off a sit-on-top, so if you're constantly getting out of your boat, you may want to look for a sit-on-top. That being said, there are many new fishing kayaks on the market that are sit-inside hybrids, with features like a wide cockpit and high seating positions to make getting in and out of your boat as easy as a sit-on-top. As always, testing the boat you're interested in during a paddle shop's demo day is a smart way to learn what you're comfortable doing in your boat and what is going to be a pain.

For slower rivers, usually wide and with a current that is almost imperceptible until you look up from changing flies and realize you're 20 yards downstream, a wide stable boat, much like the boat that you'd use for medium-size ponds and lakes, is perfectly capable. Because a slower river is wider, you can have a longer boat that will still be able to turn and get you up and down the river faster. A boat that is 12 feet long and around 30 inches wide will give you a nice balance of speed and stability. Having a keel is still a good idea, as you'll be able to track nicely when paddling up or down current and you won't need to have the maneuverability of a round-bottom boat, like you would for faster currents.

There is also a good chance that a much wider boat, all the way up to 36 inches, would work just as fine on slow-enough rivers, as you'd be fishing much like you would on a pond. Being able to stand and cast will make your life easier on the water, and kayak fly fishing becomes much more enjoyable. If you're going to be standing, a sit-on-top will give you the most stability for sight casting, seeing the fish before you make a cast, and will allow you to climb back into your boat should an object in the river like a rock or sneaky current seam sneak up on you.

No matter how slow a river is flowing, you should always keep your head on a swivel and pay close attention to your surroundings when paddling or fishing in moving water. Anglers tend to be the most at risk because they're so focused on casting, changing lures, and catching fish that they sometimes do not see the little branch sticking up out of the water. A good friend of mine who's a professional fly tier and a very experienced kayak fly fisherman, Pat Cohen, was fishing on a slow-moving creek in Vermont when he unknowingly got his boat stuck broadside, perpendicular to the current, and was flipped over before he knew what was going on. The current underwater was much stronger than it was at the surface and he was dragged straight down to the river bottom, even though he was wearing his PFD. Luckily he was able to quickly get back to the surface and into his boat before getting into more serious trouble. He still doesn't trust that river, and he's become a much more aware paddler and angler when fishing in moving water.

Some of the best fishing I've ever experienced has been fishing rivers with current fast enough that it required some paddling skill and technique, but slow enough that you could fish nearly the entire length of the river. These rivers with current in the middle range of flow speed vary greatly in size, from small backwoods creeks to rivers that are a quarter mile wide.

A mild keel, something that is not sharp or overly pronounced but is strong enough for you to feel it when you try to turn and doesn't let you spin freely, is the perfect feature for a medium-flow river. This will allow you to precisely ferry across the river to get to an eddy on the opposite bank and will help to keep you straight on course when paddling with the current, but the boat is still loose enough for you to spin it into an eddy to take a break or start fishing.

Pat Cohen hangs on for a sleigh ride as a 25-pound carp drags him around the Mohawk River in upstate New York. Balance is key to casting and fishing from a kayak, but most important if you want to fight the fish standing up.

When testing the stability of your potential river runner for medium flows, check for a primary stability that feels sturdy, but not solid like concrete. You want something that you'll be able to cast a fly rod, reach behind you to grab gear, and paddle without falling over on edge or accidentally tipping yourself. You'll also want the primary stability to be loose enough that you can tilt your hips to use the boat's edges in order to spin into an eddy and properly lean for ferrying. That's where the correct amount of secondary stability comes into play. Once you've pushed the boat on edge and through its primary stability, you should have enough secondary stability for it to feel solid and not want to flip at the first easy tilt, like a jonboat. You'll want to be able to tilt the boat on each edge, on each side of the kayak, but still feel like your balance is firm, with no risk of tipping.

Make sure to test the primary and secondary stability of your boat both before you buy it and after you've made the deal. You'll want to be comfortable with the stability and be confident that you know how far you need to tilt to get past its primary stability, where the secondary stability starts, and most importantly, know for a fact how far you can tilt before the secondary stability stops. Because once you've tilted past your secondary stability on moving water, you'll go over. That's why we always rig our gear to flip, tying down whatever doesn't float that we don't want to lose, especially in moving water.

Many sit-inside kayaks also lend themselves to river fishing, but where they shine is when the current starts to speed up and you need to start adding a few more experienced moves to your paddling repertoire. When the current picks up, there are usually more obstacles lying in the river, either at or above the surface, that you will have to avoid using proper paddling technique and, of course, the correct hull design.

A shorter boat, no bigger than 10 feet, is perfect for being capable of eddy turns, ferrying across the river in current, or just dodging rocks or sweepers, which is what paddlers call downed trees that stick out in the current. In the paddle shop, flip your proposed river-running boat over and look at the bottom of the hull for the design features. A strong keel will prevent you from spinning the boat too quickly to get into an eddy, the slow-moving water behind an obstacle like a rock, or around other obstacles in the river; therefore, look for a boat that has either a round bottom or very close to it.

You'll want a boat narrow enough to produce enough speed to get through eddy lines, the seams of swirling current that lie between an eddy and the main river; ferry across the river, moving laterally across the river without moving downstream; and bust through holes, should the water start moving fast enough to create rapids. A hole—or souse hole, as it is also called—occurs when fast-moving water passes over a rock and the water is forced to go straight down to the bottom and beneath the water that is directly downstream. The faster the current, the bigger the hole will become, with the space between the rock and the downstream water becoming bigger and bigger.

Most river boats are rotomolded but will still be lighter in weight than a lake or ocean fishing kayak, as they are shorter in length. If the river is fast enough, you may need to purchase a whitewater kayak, which are sit-inside kayaks that require you to use a skirt and know how to perform a whitewater roll. Some kayak fly anglers who also run whitewater are known to paddle through the rapids and then open their skirt and start rock hopping in order to fish the tailouts and pools with their fly rod.

There are now new fishing kayaks that are sit-on-tops but with a hull design very similar to a whitewater kayak, which allows you to paddle in rapids and strong current and make the same maneuvers as you would in a whitewater kayak without being strapped in with a skirt. This means that you don't need to learn to roll, although it's a great skill to have and a lot of fun, probably a lot more fun once you learn how to properly perform one. It also means that you can climb right back on your boat after you flip, just like you would on a lake or pond sit-on-top. Some of these sit-on-top whitewater kayaks also feature thigh straps, which allow you to perform a roll without a skirt, as you have a similar amount of control and connection to the boat as you do with a skirt, although not nearly as much as a properly fitting sit-inside whitewater kayak.

Inshore and Ocean

Oh, saltwater . . . the siren's call to many fly anglers that causes them to try fishing from a kayak, including me. I started kayak fishing in order to access more of the saltwater flats and bays that surround my childhood home, and I still haven't had my fill of the ocean. I even have a tattoo on my chest that speaks to the profound effect that the big, deep blue has had on me, which reads "Salt in my blood, sand in my bones." The salt part is actually true—the same salinity level that is in our oceans is also in our blood. We're meant to be out there, drifting along the water's surface, the ocean breeze blowing at our backs, searching for giant, beautiful, and powerful fish.

Choosing the right boat for saltwater is easier done by deciding which kind of saltwater fishing you'll be doing, of which there are two varieties: inshore and offshore. Inshore—the saltwater flats, the skinny water—is best for kayak fly fishing because you can sight fish and pick out your targets before casting to them and then, hopefully, watch them chase your fly and eat it. Battle ensues. It's why I picked up a fly rod in the first place. Many people are amazed the first time they see saltwater flats, which occur when the tide pulls most of the water out to sea and leaves some sandbars dry and others with only a foot or two, or even less, of water on other sandbars, or sand flats. Bait gathers on these shallow-water havens and so do hungry fish that are forever following their prey.

The right fishing kayak will allow you to stalk these skinny-water flats silently and offer you the best chance at seeing a fish or a school of fish before they see you. The reason many kayak anglers fish in these small plastic boats is because bigger boats like center consoles and skiffs are too large or require too much draft, the measurement of water that it takes in order to float the boat itself, in order to actually be able to float along the flats. A kayak, however, requires very little water to float, sometimes only a few inches with certain kayaks, which means you can stalk the flats throughout the entire tide cycle, no matter how shallow the water gets. Many people are surprised a big, 25-pound fish will be in such skinny water, but as long as there is enough water to cover their backs, and there is enough of a food source present, you're likely to see fish.

A wide fishing kayak is required in order to stand and spot a school of fish, or signs of fish, before they see you. Many times, even

A properly loaded fly rod will ensure a smoother, longer cast that will land correctly, not pile the line on top of the fly. Pairing the right kayak with your balance level allows you to focus on your casting, not your balance.

across a big expansive flat, you won't notice a fish until it is directly on top of you, unless you're actively standing on top of your kayak and searching for fish. A kayak that measures 34 inches wide is stable enough for you to stand comfortably all day and paddle or pole while looking for fish. Many anglers, myself included, look for kayaks that are stable enough for you to replace your seat with a cooler and stand on top of the cooler in order to reach a higher vantage point and spot fish sooner. The higher you are, the more likely you'll be able to spot fish, which is why you see guides throughout the world using flats skiffs with high sight-fishing platforms that perch the guide 4 or 5 feet above the boat's deck.

Although sit-insides are great for long distances, as they are used most often in sea kayaking and kayak touring, because standing and spotting fish is so important—absolutely crucial to the success of the day, in fact—a sit-on-top is better suited for inshore fishing. Many times, either on the way to or from the flats as well as on days when the weather rolls in or you have to battle wakes from bigger boats, a sit-on-top's scupper holes will prevent you from swamping, or filling with water. As a reminder, scupper holes, the holes located throughout the hull, allow water to pass freely through the boat. They also allow the boat to float higher on top of the water's surface, as they add buoyancy, giving you a better vantage point to spot fish.

Much like the stability needed for a big lake, the right balance of primary and secondary stability is all about finding a hull design that will give you confidence but is not so solid that it is impossible to flip over, should you fall in the drink. The primary stability should be strong enough that you can stand tall and look for fish, as well as fly cast your maximum distance without being worried about falling in. There should also be enough secondary stability that, should you need to tilt the boat on edge to paddle down the face of a wave or correct your tracking angle when paddling in the wind, you still have enough balance to remain upright.

Often the flats are not directly next to the put-in, the place where you launch your kayak, so a boat that is 34 inches wide and no wider will allow you to be fast enough to get across the bay or to a faraway flat in a decent amount of time. That's also why longer boats, around 14 or 16 feet, are better suited to the flats, because you'll have the deck space needed to stand comfortably and store all of the gear necessary for a long day of cruising, but also enough speed to paddle far distances. A boat with a good amount of flare at the bow, where the sides of the kayak are extending beyond the gunwales of the rest of the boat, will allow the oncoming chop of boat wakes or wind to be deflected rather than washing over the bow and on top of you.

Having a strong, well-defined keel will allow the angler to paddle hard against strong tides or currents and will prevent the boat from constantly turning side to side in the wind. Wind is a very big factor on the saltwater flats, both paddling in it and trying to fish in it. It seems that wind is a constant when fishing skinny water, except on very rare occasions when the fish gods look down upon you and offer up some relief. It's on those rare windless days that you see the raw beauty of the fishery come alive, spotting every crab, every baitfish, and every fish wherever you look, sometimes even a good distance away.

A keel will prevent the wind from spinning your boat while paddling or fishing, but another design feature to look for is low gunwales, or sides, of the boat. The higher the sides of the boat rise above the water, the more the wind will be able to grab a hold of and push around the boat. I've fished in boats with sides so high that sometimes I could only get a single cast out before having to readjust with a few paddle strokes. With lower sides, the wind will have less real estate to push on, allowing you to track straighter giving you more time to cast and sight fish when not paddling.

Even small saltwater fish are a worthy opponent for a fly rod—they're just as feisty as the big ones. Wider fishing kayaks allow you to target a wide array of species, no matter the size of the fish.

Many times you'll have to paddle against, or with, strong tides that will almost make you feel like you're paddling in a river, especially when surf, no matter how light, is involved. If your boat is hard to turn easily, the wave is less likely to spin you, but you want enough control that should you start to spin, you'll have the ability to right your direction. A nice, sharp bow and keel combination will not only keep you tracking straight, no matter the conditions, but will also help you cut through the chop and waves you're likely to experience in saltwater.

Deck space is prime real estate in any kind of standup fishing, but the ideal setup for inshore fishing is a roomy cockpit with plenty of room for your feet to stand and comfortably adjust, without stepping on deck rigging or hatch covers. Some of the really stable fishing kayaks currently on the market are so good that you can actually take a few steps or turn around in the cockpit while standing, which allows you more space to leave your line coiled at your feet without getting tangled. More space for your feet to adjust also prevents foot pain, as I learned the hard way on one of my earlier boats that required my feet to stay in the exact same position the entire time I was standing, as there was no other space to put them, which caused them to ache after even a short day on the water.

Stalking the flats and searching for signs of fish is a game of patience, so that usually means long days on the water, sometimes multiple tide cycles, in order to hook up on tougher days. Enough deck space and hatches for you to store essential or emergency gear is crucial. Multiple hatches allow you to store important gear, such as emergency gear, within reach and a pair of dry backup clothing that you hope to not need in a hatch farther away from the cockpit. Since you're likely to be far away from the launch, enough room to store a lunch and water, maybe in a cooler, and an extra paddle is very helpful. A large rear tankwell, the space behind the seat, is a great place to store your tackle or your cooler, as well as quick-access items like pliers, lip gripper tools, or additional rods in rod holders.

Although inshore fishing lends itself much better to kayak fly fishing than offshore fishing does, as offshore fishing usually consists of vertical jigging with conventional fishing gear or blind casting with spinning gear and usually with live bait, a fly rod can still be an effective tool. Since offshore, sometimes up to a few miles from shore, you're fishing in much deeper water, even hundreds of feet deep, some specialized techniques are needed in order to fish with a fly rod.

When it comes to the right boat for offshore fishing, it can be very similar to the kayak you'd use when fishing inshore, if not the exact same boat. The same principles still apply, wanting a stable boat that will allow you to battle big, strong fish; enough deck space to carry a lot of gear, both fishing and safety; and the right balance of width and speed to be fast. Since fishing offshore requires much more paddling than inshore, often miles compared to yards from shore, a boat that is long, up to 18 feet, and skinnier, 30 inches or under, is best, as it will give you the most speed for eating up the miles. Fishing offshore usually also means battling higher swells and waves or windy conditions, so standup fishing is not used as much; therefore, you can get away with fishing from a much skinnier boat than you would use offshore.

Other Boats: Standup Paddleboards, Pedals, Inflatables, Motors, and Canoes

While the standard fishing kayak can be a valuable tool and one that has been proven to work for the modern kayak fly angler, that doesn't mean that other types of craft won't excel just as well and get you onto more fish. It all depends on your personal style and the types of challenges you are looking to overcome.

The popularity of standup paddleboards (SUPs) has skyrocketed in the last few years, becoming one of the fastest-growing water sports around. With the rise in popularity of SUP paddling and recreation, especially SUP yoga, enterprising kayak and fly anglers are, of course, going to look at a paddleboard and say, "Yeah, I think I could catch some fish from that."

SUP fly fishing can excel in any type of fishery, from backwoods ponds to offshore and everything in between. Whatever environment you're used to fishing in, try fishing from a paddleboard to increase the difficulty and make what may have become stale more interesting. There are many new boards on the market that have been designed specifically for fishing, some with accessory mounts already included or other types of rigging that allows anglers to store gear, like seat accessories, cooler tie-downs, gear bungees, and more.

When looking for a board of your own for SUP fly fishing, look for a stable board that will allow you to cast comfortably without worrying about tipping. The same design principles apply to length and width as they do with fishing kayaks, with a short and wider board being more stable and a skinnier and longer board being faster. Most manufacturers offer an all-around board that is ideal for those who are new to balancing on a standup paddleboard, but is still long enough and fast enough to paddle well. These are the best boards to start fly fishing from, as they will be the most forgiving when trying to cast and balance at the same time, but zippy enough that you won't feel like you're trying to paddle a barge.

Since most boards are so lightweight, it is easy to pick one up and hike into your favorite put-in or backwoods pond. Although you can load up these boards and really take advantage of their high weight capacity, because there are no hatches and unnecessary rigging, they lend themselves best to minimalist fishing styles—anglers who are looking for a bare-bones approach to catching more fish.

My favorite target for SUP fishing is inshore, specifically striped bass, as the supreme stealth of a standup paddleboard lends itself perfectly to stalking the flats. I look for a board that is simple, with a handful of mounts for tying down my cooler for a higher vantage point, as well as a pair of bungees to store a rain jacket and a fly box, and another single bungee for holding my rod or paddle while I'm fishing. With this simple setup I'm able to float in the skinniest water and can explore endless backwater estuary systems, hopping from one channel to the next, and even surf the waves on the way back to the launch if the fish aren't cooperating.

On the other end of the spectrum, the latest advancement in fishing kayak design has made pedal kayaks extremely popular among kayak anglers. The most popular pedal kayaks are wide, almost rectangular, and have a high weight capacity so you can pack all of your gear and electronics on board for a full day of fishing. Much like a bass boat that professional anglers use in bass tournaments, these boats have multiple rigging capabilities perfect for loading down with electronics, as your legs do the work and you don't have to worry about paddling all that weight with your upper body.

Getting lower while you present your fly can increase your chances of remaining stealthy and not spooking nearby fish with your passing shadow.

Pointing your rod tip on the final cast will ensure your fly line unfolds properly and allows you to present your fly as accurately as possible.

Since these boats are known for being so stable, they make a great platform for kayak fly fishing, with the proper rigging and precautions. Because the pedals stick up from the center of the hull and are located within reach of your feet when sitting down, when you're standing up, the pedals will be directly at your feet, in the way of your fly line. If you don't do something to prevent your line from tangling in the pedals before and after every cast, you're going to experience the most frustrating day of fly fishing in your life. All it takes to prevent the tangling, though, is a stripping basket at your feet, basically a bucket, either cloth or plastic, that collects the line that you are peeling off of your reel so that it can shoot easily and not get tangled. If you don't want to use a stripping basket and want something a little more streamlined or easier to pack away in a pocket or PFD, a simple towel or big T-shirt placed over the pedals will prevent the line from tangling.

Inflatable boat designs, whether they're kayaks, canoes, or standup paddleboards, are also becoming more and more popular, especially for people who need a boat that stores in small places like a closet inside an apartment, or need to transport the boat in the trunk of a small car. Modern inflatable designs have advanced the performance of these boats, making many of them fun to paddle and stiff enough to not bend and feel like you're paddling a pool toy; some even feature fishing accessories. Most rod holder and fishing kayak accessory manufacturers offer solutions for mounting rod holders and electronics to your inflatable boat, which allows anglers the same fishing capabilities as their buddy's hard plastic kayak, but in an easy-to-store inflatable version.

If you need a boat that inflates and can be stored most anywhere, look for one that will inflate to a very rigid platform that won't bend when you paddle or fish inside of it. Also, some inflatable boats now feature a hard plastic bow or keel, which translates to a boat that will cut through the water better, rather than bending to the pressure of oncoming current or waves. A boat that performs like it's not an inflatable and reacts to paddle input just as well, or almost as well, as a hard plastic boat is the best way to achieve the best of both worlds.

Another benefit of inflatable boats is that they tend to ride very high in the water, as they are much more buoyant than a hard boat, and therefore can give you a drier ride. Inflatable boats also tend to be lighter in weight, which is great for anglers who need to portage their boats to the water or be able to lift the boat on top of a car or truck.

Motors are also becoming more and more popular in the kayak fishing world and seem to be drawing more interest from other anglers throughout the different styles of fishing. Bass anglers especially seem interested in the newest fishing kayaks that feature motors, but fly anglers could also use motor systems to increase the time they have for fishing. The great thing about motor systems is that you free up your hands so you can focus on fishing, and this can allow you to cast and fish without constantly needing to readjust with your paddle.

The author's wife, Jennie Duchesney, admires one of the many locals before setting off of dry land in search of striped bass on the flats. No matter what boat you choose, don't forget to stop and look at your surroundings.

Many manufacturers are starting to offer motored versions of their already-popular fishing kayak models—meaning the kayak design is the same as the paddle version, so it will paddle and fish the same as the non-motor version—but most of the time the new model is slightly larger. A designer of one of the motor-driven kayaks said the new fishing kayak was an inch bigger everywhere than the old kayak, as in width, height, length, etc. Weight, however, tends to be drastically different in the motored versions, as all that equipment is a significant addition to the hull.

Rather than looking for the latest advancements in plastic and design, some anglers like to go the traditional route and fish from a canoe, one of my favorite boats ever to be designed. As one of the oldest boat designs in existence, canoes have been perfected over hundreds of years, and there is nothing quite like paddling a well-made canoe through the water. An icon of the North, there is a rich aesthetic quality of fly fishing from a canoe that really can't be matched. The sight of someone paddling in a wooden canoe, casting a fly rod for rising trout, may be one of the finest sights that you can behold, especially if that angler is you and you're about to catch a fish.

One of the great pleasures of fly fishing from a canoe lies in the simplicity of the boat and the great lack of points where your line can get snagged before a cast. If you're paddling solo, as many fly anglers who fish from canoes tend to do, you have a wide open hull at your feet where your line can collect. Many people who are unfamiliar with canoes, or have spent just a minimal amount of time paddling inside one, are likely to think of canoes as unstable, but like all boats, it's just a matter of getting used to the primary and secondary stability of the craft, which will then make you realize a canoe is one of the most stable boats you'll ever paddle in. Why else would paddlers choose a canoe to run through whitewater?

The primary stability of a canoe is where most people decide that they don't like fishing, or even paddling, inside one. With a softer primary stability, canoes are capable of being tilted to one side or the other and carving through the water in order to make a tighter or more aggressive turn. Many times, especially if the canoe has a strong keel, paddlers will feel like they are falling from one side to the other when tilting a canoe on edge, but that is the canoe tilting past its primary stability and engaging the secondary.

The secondary stability is why the canoe has excelled for hundreds of years. If you're properly placed in the center of the boat and properly tilting with your hips, keeping your head over the center of the boat and not leaning your body to the side, it would be difficult to overextend its stability and flip. There is even a fun game that you can play with a partner in a tandem canoe called "gunwale bobbing." Each player stands on opposite ends of the canoe, balancing on the gunwales, and take turns bobbing their end into the water. Whichever paddler stays in the boat the longest wins. After one game of gunwale bobbing with two players with good balance, any naysayer who thinks canoes are not stable will be amazed.

When choosing a canoe to fish from with a fly rod, I look for a boat that will paddle well solo and tandem, giving me the most bang for my buck and the best chance at a stable fly-fishing platform. Some wider canoes will even allow you to stand and sight cast, once you've become accustomed to fishing from a canoe and have acquired the right feel for the stability. Whether you're fishing solo or with a partner, watch your balance and make sure you're not swaying from side to side while casting, causing the boat to rock. This will ensure your cast has proper technique and you don't fall into the water.

TESTED ON ANIMALS
4x4

CHAPTER 2

Choosing the Right Gear

Kayak fly anglers have a problem with gear, and that's because they have so much of it available to them. Not only do we have piles and piles of fly-fishing gear, but we also need kayaking and paddling gear and then other general fishing gear like electronics, tools, nets, clothing, and countless other things. Yes, we need it. And this is a good problem.

It seems that every kayak fly angler goes through the same progression. They start out with what they can afford to see if they like the sport, which they usually do because of its low cost of entry, especially when compared to a $60,000 bass boat, and then they get hooked. Once they're hooked, a new rod, a shiny new carbon fiber paddle, and a more comfortable PFD are bought without a thought. And then there's the new crate system, new fish finder, and matching fishing clothes, made in the fanciest synthetic material that can be found in this known universe—maybe they even get them custom made, with the logos of sponsors and the angler's last name across the back and all over the sleeves, of course.

Once they've attained a certain level of gear obsession, the purging starts. At the point where they have enough gear to create two, or maybe even three, complete outfits that would fully get an angler ready to hit the water, that's when they realize they probably have enough gear. Not only is this essential to finding out what gear you like, the tools you need, and the brands you trust, but it also helps encourage others to try out the sport.

Take your time getting ready and tying on a fly before you hit the water—you can then start fishing as soon as you see signs of fish.

Noisy topwater poppers can attract bass and other species, though they are harder to pull off the water during the start of your cast. Fishing with anglers who are better than you will teach you the little tricks you won't find anywhere else.

Fly fishing and paddling both have a long history of mentoring, with more-experienced anglers taking new ones under their casting arm and showing them the way, giving them old gear that they can learn with and teaching them everything they know. Without this essential step in every kayak fly angler's progression, the sport wouldn't be exploding in popularity as much as it is right now. I encourage every angler to buy at least two of every essential item, as long as it doesn't put a strain on the bank account, of course. This plan give you a backup, should you break your primary rod or paddle, but it also lets you bring along a friend who's never done it before.

When I started kayak fishing, I couldn't wait to get off work and start rigging and re-rigging my kayak with the latest gadget that I ordered online or picked up from the local paddle shop, which I researched for hours and hours until I was sure that I'd chosen the exact tool for the job. I'd tinker away at building out the perfect kayak crate, loaded up with different rod holders, and then add even more rod holders and mounts throughout the deck of my kayak so that I could troll at any angle and switch positions or sides of the boat. I even added an extra rod holder in case I didn't want to put the rod back in the trolling rod holder while I tied on a new lure or made a quick adjustment stroke with my paddle. When I was on the water, if I wasn't casting or reeling, I was moving things around, looking in my crate for the next lure that I wanted to throw, making sure my tools were where they needed to be should I hook up to a fish, and making sure my paddle had a spot to rest while I was fishing so that it didn't fall into the drink, even though I'd also added a paddle leash so it couldn't get away. Frankly, it was all too much.

I look at my current bare-bones kayak gear and the pile of gear beside it that I no longer bring, and I never feel like I wasted time or money because friends use it all the time. It's as much their gear as it is mine, and they know it. My friends and I were at the bar one Friday night this past summer, making plans and checking the weather for a big motorcycle

Doubling up the amount of line you pull through the guides ensures you'll have enough to tie on a fly with ease. This will cut down the amount of time it takes you to rig up, getting you on the water faster.

ride up into the mountains that weekend. I noticed the tides were perfect for a launch at sunrise for striped bass off the local beach and, even though we were currently at the bar drinking and not thinking about the morning, I suggested we hit the water before jumping on the bikes and hitting the throttle. Immediately all of them said no, except one guy. He'd grown up fishing with his dad here and there—his dad even owned two kayaks—but he'd never tried kayak fishing and never caught a striped bass, and it seemed he was curious to find out why I was so obsessed.

"Are you sure you have enough gear for the both of us?" he asked, taking another sip of his beer. "I've got nothing."

"Just show up with your dad's kayak and wear a hat and a bathing suit," I said. "I'll get the rest."

The next morning, as soon as he pulled up to the beach parking lot right beside the water, I had a pair of high-quality polarized sunglasses, a UV-protection sun shirt, and a pair of water shoes for him to put on, and he asked, "Why won't my shades work?"

"Put these on," I said.

As soon as he looked up with the new shades and peered into the water just below us, he started smiling and nodding. The more he looked down into the water, seeing farther and deeper into the ocean than he ever could before with his cheap shades, he understood why I spent so much money on good polarized sunglasses. As he was taking his dad's kayak off his truck, I laid out a good paddle for him, as well as an inflatable PFD that would be more comfortable, and attached a lanyard with a few essential tools to the base of his kayak's seat. I placed a rod, already rigged with a pink soft plastic on a jig head, beside the paddle and threw a container with two other styles of plastics and a few spare jig heads on the ground beside the rod.

After fishing all day and seeing a few fish, but nothing of size, we washed the saltwater off of the gear with a jug of water from the back of my truck and started packing everything away neatly. He started to take off the shirt and sunglasses, but I stopped him and told him to keep them. I knew there would be a next time that we'd go fishing, and I knew that if he already had the right gear that it'd be much sooner.

You don't have to give away all your gear to your buddies, but letting them at least borrow higher-quality gear than what they'd likely start out with without you lets them try the sport without being at a disadvantage. I feel the same philosophy is true for new anglers, no matter their age—whether they are your peers, older friends, or your kids, trying out a new sport with poorly performing, cheap gear is more likely to make them not enjoy themselves and give up on it too quickly. If someone has a great experience with a new activity, whether it be kayak fly fishing, skiing, whitewater paddling, or any sport there is, they are more likely to give it another shot and get excited about the sport. Bad gear will only hold them back and is more likely to discourage them, so make sure your backups are of a quality that you'd want to fish with and you'll soon have a new fishing buddy who will let you borrow his gear. Maybe.

Wearing an inflatable PFD, or personal flotation device, can be a more comfortable option for anglers who want to fish flat water for trophy fish. It's tempting to load up your gear on the front of a PFD, but make sure it's still functional and comfortable.

New gadgets are a lot of fun, as much fun as rigging up your kayak or researching which PFD will give you the most range of motion or which paddle is lighter, and even almost as much fun as catching fish. Ask any fly-fishing instructor, outfitter, or guide and they're likely to tell you the same thing: Watching people catch fish for the first time is as good a rush as catching a fish yourself. When that new person is your best buddy who's been curious about kayak fly fishing for a long time but has been hesitant to pull the trigger on the new gear outfit, that rush will be even greater. So don't feel bad about buying that new rod. You need it, your new buddies need it, and so does the sport.

Fly Rods

When it comes to the right fly rod for kayak fly fishing, there's a battle that's been going on for decades throughout the industry over what's best: fast or slow. Back in the day when fly fishing was mostly done by old guys with funny hats on trout streams, slow fiberglass rods were all they fished with. Once saltwater fishing started to influence the market and anglers began slinging bigger flies to bigger fish, along with bigger flies to freshwater fish like largemouth bass or even musky, faster graphite rods started to become more and more popular. Whichever side you choose, fast or slow, it all depends on your fishing style and your personal preference.

I love casting a fast-action rod, the fastest one I can get my hands on, but I have a friend with a new custom-made, slow-action fiberglass rod. We can fish side by side all day long, happily catching fish in the same stream and shooting casts similar distances with similar accuracy, but with a completely different style. After we got off the water on the day he first showed me his new custom rod, which is a beautiful work of art and feels as electric in your hands as your high school prom date, I decided that I wouldn't want to fish with it. I'll admit that I enjoyed casting it—I even cast it accurately, with some impressive distance that nearly surprised me—but I still wouldn't buy one. It was just too slow.

No matter the rod speed you decide is best for your style, which could also change depending on where you fish or your mood that day, something that doesn't change is the length that you should look for in a kayak fly-fishing rod. Any angler fishing with a spinning rod in a kayak runs the risk of fishing with a rod that is too short and not being able to reach around the bow of the kayak in order to allow a fish to run to the other side of the boat, without breaking the line against your kayak. Most fly rods, on the other hand, are over 7 feet, the usual distance recommended for a spin angler while fishing from a kayak, so it becomes a matter of where you are fishing. When it comes to fishing in boats, many drift boat guides would say that a longer rod is better, because a longer rod keeps the line farther up in the air, away from the other anglers in the boat and out of the way of the oars.

Make sure your fly rod's guides are lined up and straight—that way your cast will be accurate. No matter what style of rod you choose, it's these little details that often benefit beginner anglers the most.

Guides in tighter trout streams would suggest a more nimble, shorter rod, something that is more accurate and lighter for hiking up and down the river. Big tailwater river guides and saltwater guides would recommend a longer, faster rod so that you can throw casts farther and have more control over presentation and mending.

In general, shorter rods will have a lighter feel to them, and longer rods will feel slightly heavier, as the weight has to extend farther away from the central balance point, which should be at the rod's grip. Even two rods that are nearly identical in weight and only 6 inches different in length may feel significantly heavier, depending on their design, of course, all due to the length. Shorter rods also feel more accurate and are better for throwing casts under overhanging branches or into deeply cut riverbanks, as they can be cast sidearm more easily. Longer rods have the benefit of greater mending control, as the rod is in contact with more line. A longer rod will also act as a larger lever on which the fly line can travel, meaning you tend to have greater control of your line when making a longer cast with more line in the air, and will also make your roll casts more powerful.

When you're trying to decide which rod length is best for your fishing needs, look at the fishery in which you intend to fish. If the casting is tighter and more technical, or there are a lot of overhanging branches or bushes that you could get hung up on, you may want to start out with a shorter rod. If you're fishing a big saltwater flat or freshwater pond, with no worries of getting your backcast fouled by a tree, you can start with a longer rod and keep your line out of the way of your rigging and camera poles that are all around your kayak. I'd suggest starting with the standard-length rod that is the most popular and the easiest to find at any fly shop: the 9-footer. Nine feet is the length that is the most recommended and therefore the most used for general fly fishing. If you feel you don't have enough precision, try out a smaller rod, or if you need more distance, try out a longer rod. Either way, make sure you try out multiple rods, in multiple styles and lengths, at the fly shop before you buy anything. The right-length rod that you think you need may be different than the rod that fits your casting style the best.

When it comes to fighting fish in a kayak, the design of your fly rod has everything to do with whether or not you land that fish. Since you have less leverage while sitting down in a kayak, you need a rod that is designed to back you up with some extra punch, but also to protect light leaders and not break your line every time you try to land a fish.

Where and when a rod loads up on a fish dictates how an angler can use the rod. Most fly anglers working technical presentations or finesse tactics will choose a slower-power or slower-action rod because they tend to load only at a full bend. This means you can twitch and move a fly on the end of your line subtly, even when aggressively twitching your rod tip. It also means that a fish can pick up the fly and start swimming off with it without your noticing any tension on the line and spit the hook. Many times, especially when fishing skittish fish or in tough, usually cold conditions, an

Practice your cast both standing up and sitting down until you figure out your own casting style. When standing, make sure you keep your body from the waist down completely still and only use your arms and the fly rod's action to cast.

angler will want more time between when the fish picks up the fly with a soft bite and the moment when a hook set is needed. With a softer rod, a fish will never know the fly is attached to a leader connected to an angler, whereas a faster-action or faster-power rod will immediately react to the tension of a fish picking up the fly. Slow-action rods, like the increasingly popular old-fashioned fiberglass, are perfect for these tough fishing conditions or tricky fish.

More aggressive tactics require a rod that will quickly load when a fish strikes. Anglers fishing with streamers or weighted flies will want a rod that can set the hook with immediate input from the angler. These fast-action rods will have power under less of a bend—sometimes only a quarter bend of the rod will pick up the line or set the hook on a fish. The power in these rods comes from closer to the tip than a slow-action rod, which only has power down the midsection of the rod. Anglers fishing for species with hard mouths like saltwater fish or big *Esox* (northern pike and musky), basically any fish that requires a strip-set, will most likely want a fast-action rod. A strip-set is a valuable technique for fly fishing for bigger game. Instead of lifting the rod tip to set the hook, an angler will rear back on the rod with a side angle and pull the line tight on the fish with their line hand, or the hand not holding the rod. This adds greater pressure to the hook point and drives the hook into the tougher mouths of these bigger fish.

Fly Reels, Lines, and Leaders

Start fly fishing from a kayak and you'll see that your gear takes serious abuse, and nothing takes more than your fly reels. Imagine for a moment the average day in the life of a reel used by a kayak fly angler. The second it's seated to the rod and strung up, it's placed in the seat of a kayak or leaned up against the truck while the angler finishes the task of getting his gear ready for a day on the water. While the angler drags the kayak through the mud, sand, or dirt, or maybe he's an evolved angler and uses a kayak cart to get his boat to the water, but even still, the reel is being bounced around on hard plastic and runs the risk of falling out and landing in the dirt, bouncing off a rock, or getting sand lodged inside it. What about putting the rod in a rod holder and protecting it while getting to the water? Since fly rods are longer than other rods, it's likely that the average angler waits to put the rod in the holder until he's ready to get into the water, for fear of breaking the rod's tip in a tree or causing the long rod to wave back and forth too harshly while the kayak is being dragged.

Once the angler pushes off from dry land and the rod is in the rod holder, safe for the time being, the reel is likely to get constantly splashed, either by waves or by every errant paddle stroke. No big deal if the angler is fishing in freshwater, but if he or she is in saltwater, cruising the flats or heading offshore, that means the salt is seeping in with the intent of corroding every piece of metal it can get its hands on. While the angler is looking for fish, making paddle corrections, landing or releasing fish, or changing a fly, where is the reel placed? Either in the relative safety of the angler's lap, although that's likely covered with fish slime, water, or spilt coffee, or between the angler's legs, likely soaking in the water that has seeped into the kayak from the scupper holes and being scratched and filled with the sand or mud from the angler's feet when he stepped into the boat. Any time the angler is casting to a fish and needs to make a quick paddle correction to dodge a rock in the river or battle the wind on the saltwater flats or on a pond, the rod is dropped to the boat as quickly and carefully as possible, but what ends up happening is the reel takes most of the shock of the fall, as it is the lowest part of the rod when it drops from the hand.

A high-quality, large-arbor reel will ensure you have plenty of line and backing storage and enough drag power to stop big fish in their tracks.

For these reasons, and not even thinking about actually handling a fish yet, which is also important, whenever anglers ask me which fly reel is best for kayak fly fishing, I always suggest the strongest reel they can possibly find. Whether fishing saltwater or fresh, I always urge anglers to look for a sealed drag. When a reel's drag is not sealed, the internal gears and drag mechanisms, regardless of what kind of drag system they use, are open and vulnerable to sand, dirt, salt, and grime getting in there, into the weakest part of the reel, and causing damage. A sealed drag, on the other hand, prevents damage to its weakest components and lets an angler fish nearly worry-free of reel damage.

Once you've found a reel that can withstand the endless abuse of kayak fly fishing, it's time to see which reel boasts the power and strength needed to fight a fish from a little plastic boat. Because kayaks are so light and can be dragged around or spun by a fish, which many anglers call a "Nantucket sleigh ride" or just "sleigh ride," you have to set your drag differently than you would when fishing on land or from a much bigger boat that the fish cannot influence. If you're fishing from a platform that cannot be moved by the fish, you must set your drag so the fish is allowed to run freely to prevent breaking your line or causing enough tension to break your delicate leader. When fishing from a kayak, on the other hand, anglers can set their drag a little tighter than they normally would, which lets the kayak become part of the drag system. Now instead of the fish just fighting against the strength in your arms and the pressure from the reel, the fish must do that *and* pull the weight of your kayak through the water. This is why fighting a fish from a kayak can be so exciting, because you and your kayak are both a bigger part of the fight. Anglers fishing from a kayak are often able to tire a fish faster than they would if they were fishing from a bigger boat or from land, which means that you can get the fish revived and back in the water faster, promoting a healthier fish population, and save more time for fishing.

When it comes to setting your drag, the most common mistake that anglers make is mistrusting their own settings once they hook a fish and messing with the drag while the fish is on the line. If an angler is hooked up to a big fish that is running left and right, peeling line off the reel, and feels that the fish is taking line too easily, the worst mistake the angler can make is to touch the drag and tighten it. Tightening the drag under the pressure of a fighting fish means you have no idea what you just set that drag to and also runs the risk of causing the drag to slip, creating slack in the line and causing you to lose the fish. If you've set the drag too tight during a fight, which is the most common occurrence when messing with the drag during the fight, you're likely to lose the fish by causing your leader to break under pressure. On the other end of the spectrum, it is also possible to accidentally turn your drag knob the wrong direction and cause the drag to loosen, which would also create slack in the line, allowing the fish to spit the hook and come off.

To properly set your drag, put your rod in a rod holder and grab a scale designed to measure the weight of a fish, which usually has some sort of hook or plier-jaws at the end to hold the fish. Check the pound test of the leader that you have tied to the end of your fly line, marked on the package the leader came in. Tie a loop at the end of your leader and attach it to your scale; when you start to pull on the scale, you'll get a measurement on the pressure of the line. You should only set your drag to 20 to 25 percent of the line's breaking point—that way, no matter what a fish does, the line won't break from too much pressure. It still might break if the fish runs your line through a clump of rocks or into a stump, but that's a whole different problem. For example, if your leader is rated at 12-pound test, the scale should read 3 pounds before you hear your drag start to click, which means your reel is letting out line before the load becomes too great. If your scale is reading a

Jackson

Professional fly tier Pat Cohen gets dragged around the flats alongside the Mohawk River, New York, by a big, 25-pound carp. Having a reel that you trust will allow you to apply more pressure to a fish and end the fight sooner.

higher number before the reel is engaged, or the line breaks before your reel starts letting out line, your drag is too tight.

Remember, no matter how much the fish doesn't seem to be tiring, and no matter how tired you are, tightening the drag at the end of a fight will not bring it to an end sooner—it will just cause you to lose fish. That's why every kayak fishing guide around will tell you never to touch the drag on the rod they've handed you, whether during a fight or before one, because they've already set it perfectly to allow you to wear out each fish with just the right amount of pressure.

As I hinted above, there are certain situations that require you to increase pressure on the fish in order to keep it out of a stump or away from rocks or the main current of a river, which will cause you to lose the fish. Rather than tightening the drag and trying to reset it once the fish is backed away from the obstruction, the safest way to add a little pressure without breaking your line is to palm the reel. While the fish is making a run, or you feel it starting to dive-bomb into a mess of weeds or a submerged tree, you can cup the reel in your line hand, or the hand that is not currently holding onto the rod grip, and apply a little pressure to cause the reel to spin slower. Don't cause the reel to stop spinning completely, however, as this will surely lead to the audible "pop" of your leader breaking and the fish swimming away.

Finding the right balance of pressure when palming a reel to keep a fish out of certain structure is all about feel, and that can only come with a little luck and a lot of practice. Experience is the name of the game when learning to palm a reel, so you should practice with a friend in your front yard before heading after big fish. Properly set your drag as mentioned above, no more than 20 to 25 percent of its breaking point, and have your friend run away from you as you hold the rod, as if he were a big fish. Make sure he starts slowly so you don't snap the line before he gets up to speed. As he is running, start palming the reel lightly and learn to get a feel for how much pressure you can apply before the line breaks. Keep practicing so you can learn the limits of your line, and be sure to try out different sizes and weights of leaders so you can have a feel for any fishing situation.

Since loading the rod is the most crucial step when casting from a kayak, there are certain qualities to look for when buying the right fly lines and leaders. Even though all fly lines are scientifically engineered to cast perfectly, no rod setup or angler casts exactly the same, so buying fly line is all about finding one to match your needs and cast. Out of all the lines to start with, weight-forward fly lines and line styles known as "bug tapers" are great for loading line quickly and will be the easiest to both learn to cast from a kayak and cast the vast majority of flies that you will need. The reason these lines are called "bug tapers" is because of the type of fly that they are designed to throw, most often large wind-resistant bass bugs. These flies require more power to push them through the air, as their profile is so much larger than a traditional fly, and sometimes they are even weighted, so the lines are designed with extra weight at

Use the knot that you trust most. If you try a fancy new knot without perfecting it, you could lose the fish. The leader that you use to tie on your fly will change depending on what type of fish you're after and the conditions.

the front of the line, or part of the line closest to the fly. These could also just as well be called "kayak fishing tapers," as the heavier front of the line allows the rod to load the line more easily, perfect for casting while seated in a kayak, as you will have less leverage and space to move your fly rod and line.

When it comes to leaders, what you need depends more on your target species than being in a kayak. Longer leaders can be a little harder to cast and manage in a kayak, since you don't have room to peel out line from the tip should your line fall through the guides while you're on the water, which will eventually happen. No matter what kind of craft you're fishing from, longer leaders will likely add difficulty and frustration but are sometimes necessary to hook up. As a general rule, the spookier the target fish, the longer and lighter your leader needs to be, within the weight class for the fish. Fly lines are thick and often colored, while leaders are clear and thin. One end of your leader is tied to the end of your fly line, and the other is tied to the fly. This allows you to cast your weightless, or nearly weightless, fly with your thick and visible fly line, while the leader, nearly invisible to the fish, presents your fly to the fish without spooking it.

The most common leaders are chemically tapered, meaning that the leader starts at a certain thickness at the end connected to the fly line and then gradually gets thinner and thinner until it reaches the fly. This gradual thinning, or taper, in thickness allows the leader to properly unfurl, or unroll at the end of the cast, and present the fly in the cleanest, smoothest way possible. You can also build your own leaders by tying different sections of leader material, usually monofilament or fluorocarbon, in descending weights to create a length and weight of leader that you need to catch a certain species of fish. This allows you to customize your leaders to your exact fishery needs, or your exact casting style, for the best possible presentation, though sometimes the knots can collect debris or dirt while fishing and hinder your presentation, which is why manufacturers chemically taper their leaders for a completely smooth and seamless finish.

Leaders are often labeled with a number and the letter X, known as the "X system," to signify the weight of the leader, usually starting at 03X, the thickest and strongest at 25-pound test, and progressing to 8X, the lightest at 1.75-pound test. When buying a leader, your general formula should be to buy the strongest leader that you can while still retaining the lightness required for the fish to not see the line. To put it simply, the 03X leaders are for big game; 01X to 1X for flats species like bonefish, redfish, or striped bass; 3X to 5X for freshwater species like bass, panfish, and most trout; and then 6X to 8X for very difficult or easily spooked trout, or for very small flies.

When buying a leader, the fly shop clerk will probably talk to you about tippet or tippet material. Like the leader, tippet is designed to not be seen by the fish and can be added to the end of your leader to extend its length. I tell most beginner kayak fly anglers that tippet is great for extending the life of your leader, replenishing the length as you continually snip the end of the leader to change flies or when you break off small portions of your leader while fighting fish. While this is the most common reason I use tippet, you can also use it to increase the length of your leader when fishing for super-finicky fish, or fish that have continued to refuse your fly. Since tippet is usually the thinnest and lightest part of your leader, this is a great way to add to your leader's stealth factor. Because tippet is not tapered, but rather is the same thickness throughout, adding too much tippet at the front of your leader will reduce the gradual taper of the leader and could eventually affect your cast, causing your leader to not properly unroll in your presentation.

Outfitting and Rigging

You can spend hours and hours rigging and outfitting your new fishing kayak to get it dialed in to your exact style and needs, and often you'll continually be changing and upgrading your setup, no matter if you think you've finished it.

Working at *Kayak Angler* magazine, two articles were pitched by new kayak anglers or

Fly anglers get ready to launch in Beverly, Massachusetts, in search of big stripers at low tide. Kayak carts make the weight of your kayak less important, so you can pack on the gear and keep fishing.

new writers more than any other topic: one being a rigging how-to on building a kayak crate and loading it up with all kinds of tools, electronics, and rod holders, and the other an essay arguing that simpler is better and that you shouldn't bring everything you think you need on the water. Not only does this illustrate that all anglers go through the same internal battle when it comes to rigging, but it also points out that every angler has different needs and you have to experiment to dial in exactly what you need on the water. Also, don't be afraid to change your setup. I always suggest a rigging system that is not permanent, something that can be altered at any time—that way you can be constantly changing and evolving without worrying about committing to a new item.

When it comes to rigging, my personal style has always been minimal: I only bring what I absolutely need, nothing more and nothing less. I like to keep the deck of my kayak as clean as possible to eliminate any tangling or snagging of my fly line, and I like a big center area to stand and sight cast from. Sometimes I'll add a cooler in order to gain a higher vantage point, but often I settle for reusing or repurposing already existing items that are on my kayak and stand on the seat.

Whether you choose to live large on the water, bringing everything you could possibly ever want, or you go for a simpler setup and bring hardly anything at all, there are always ways to make your kayak more suited for fly fishing, be it snag-proofing, streamlining, or just making things a little more comfortable.

THE KAYAK CRATE

When it comes to the deck space on a fishing kayak, every square inch is at a premium. Anglers often opt for the classic kayak crate, usually a rigged-up milk crate, located in the rear tankwell, which keeps most of the gear, rods, and other tools out of the way until they are absolutely needed. Building your own crate has become part of the ritual of learning how to fish from a kayak, so much so that many kayak fishing pros have created countless articles and videos on how they designed or built their own crate. Companies have also started offering their own versions of the kayak crate, which have now become standard items on most kayak fishing rigs.

I suggest making your own crate, without watching or reading how the pros made theirs—that way your crate fits your exact needs, and you might even come up with unique and better solutions to common problems. To get started, find a common plastic milk crate, which you're likely to somehow already have in your house, though you might not know how it got there.

Many anglers like to cut out the front of the crate so that they can better access their gear, but that may limit the amount of tackle you can fit in there. Place the crate in your tankwell and take a seat on your kayak in your garage or yard. Try reaching back into the crate and accessing gear, without leaning to one side or tipping the kayak too far over and "falling in." Make sure you're wearing your PFD and whatever other gear you'll be fishing in to reenact the exact conditions you'll be facing on the water. If you can't reach your gear without

No matter how you choose to rig your boat, kayak fly fishing takes a lot of gear. Make sure your rod and reel is properly supported when you're stringing it up; otherwise, you could easily damage the rod.

tipping too far over to one side or the other, or you are straining too much to access gear, you may need to cut the front of the crate.

Next, lay out the gear and tackle boxes that you want to bring with you on the water and consolidate until they all fit into the milk crate. Standard tackle trays, available at hardware stores or fishing shops everywhere, fit into a milk crate best. Once you've filled the crate, you're only halfway done.

Next, buy PVC pipe big enough to fit all of your rod butts—buy for the largest rod you use, not the smallest—and cut them to size. Usually a foot in length is all you need to secure a rod, but most anglers measure their milk crate from top to bottom and then add 2 or 3 inches. Drill four holes into the PVC, two at the top and two at the bottom, on the side of the pipe that will rest along the crate. Use zip ties to secure the PVC pipes, as many as you want, to the milk crate for perfect rod holders that will let you store your rods or troll easily. Rod holders work best either at the back of the crate or along the sides; avoid placing them in the front, as this would limit your access to the inside of the crate. To allow the PVC rod holders to accept fly rods, cut a 1-inch slit down the center of the PVC or on one side, depending on where you want the fly reel to be located. This will allow the rod handle to sit inside the PVC pipe and the reel to sit just outside, with the reel seat located between the 1-inch slit that you made.

Many anglers decide to store their tools, like pliers, knives, nippers, or fish grippers, at the front of the milk crate. You can use paracord, cheap and available at most hardware stores, or gear retainers, either retracting or bungee, to secure your tools to the front of your crate, though quick-release systems that allow you to detach the tools for use and then resecure them afterwards are the best. When fishing from a kayak, always rig your gear, especially your expensive tools, as if you plan to flip your kayak. That way, should you flip your kayak and take an unexpected swim, you'll lose hardly any gear, if any at all, and if you're wearing a PFD and the right clothing, you can keep on fishing.

Many anglers decide they want to raise their crate off the deck of their kayak, giving them a little more space underneath the crate to store more quick-access gear and to keep things in the crate a little bit drier while fishing. To raise the crate off the deck of your kayak, run two dowel rods through the bottom of the crate, perpendicular to the kayak, one on each side of the crate. Use zip ties to secure the dowels to the crate. The ends of the dowels should fit into the pad eyes that are likely on your kayak's deck already, located on each side of the rear tankwell, but you may need to add them. You can buy them cheaply at most marine supply stores and install them with a drill and some silicone sealant in just a few minutes.

GO MINIMAL

Once you decide that this is all too much gear for you, or you end up only using one tackle box or fly box on the water, you can leave the milk crate at home and instead consolidate all of your essential flies and lures into one big tackle box and just bring that along instead. For me, being more minimal with my gear means that I can focus more time on actually fishing and finding fish, rather than trying to find the right tool or the exact lure that I'm thinking of using.

To achieve a more minimal setup, I look for things that can perform the jobs of multiple tools. For example, when I'm looking at tackle boxes, instead of bringing four different tackle trays, some for swimbaits and some for hard plastics and a separate one for flies, I carry one big tray for all of my spinning tackle and one big fly box for all of my flies. That way I know that I'll have the right flies whenever I hit the water and won't forget a box, but it also means that I won't spend too much time digging through boxes, looking for the right fly.

Harry Duchesney stands on his seat to better scan the surrounding flats in the estuaries of Cape Cod for cruising striped bass. Keeping rigging to a minimum allows a fly angler to move around and find fish more quickly.

CAMERAS

Cameras have become as big a part of kayak fishing as, well, kayaks. Lightweight, waterproof cameras are an essential part of the basic kayak fishing kit, not only for recording the fish that anglers catch, with shots of the fish being held up to the camera, which is called a "grip and grin shot," but also for recording highlight reels and full trip recaps. Many anglers have started making a name for themselves by recording their kayak fishing adventures, which helps the sport reach more audiences and grow.

For kayak fly fishing, it's essential that your camera gear doesn't interfere with your fly line and your casting, which means a clear line of sight and as few camera mounts as possible that your line can get tangled on. When I first started, I placed a tripod towards the bow of the kayak, between my feet, and secured it with a handful of bungee cords that I picked up at a hardware store. On top of that I placed a big DSLR camera with a flip-out screen, which was handy for checking focus and making sure the camera was recording. Not only was this bulky and in the way, but it also probably looked weird to other anglers.

The translucent, spiny dorsal fin of a schoolie striped bass is a beautiful sight to behold, even in the smallest fish. Having a camera within reach means you can document the everyday beauty of fly fishing from a kayak.

Look for camera poles that will attach to your kayak via base mounts, which will allow you to quickly release them to change the position on your kayak to get a new angle or to shoot your buddy, and also allow the camera poles to be easily swung out of the way for fishing and casting. The best mounts I've found allow you to lock them in place while filming or leave the pole unlocked in the base, which lets me rotate the mount 360 degrees and also change the camera angle at the pole's head. That way I can fish as I normally would, but when I catch a fish, I can swing it into view and hit "record."

ELECTRONICS

Because I mostly fish on the saltwater flats, electronics aren't a major tool in my arsenal, but I do use them for scouting purposes, or when I'm fishing in freshwater or deeper in the ocean. The key to using electronics is not relying on them so much that you hardly look up from the screen, but rather using them as an aid to know where to fish or how to fish—as in the right depth, speed, etc.—and then using your fishing skill to actually fish. I often

A portable fish finder unit with a suction-cup-mounted transducer will allow you to swap the unit from kayak to kayak in seconds. Notice the transducer wire hanging over the side of the kayak near the paddler's right foot, extending below the kayak's deck. This makes the picture on the fish finder as clear and easy to read as possible.

see anglers focusing too much on their electronics, constantly checking and rechecking their equipment for any slight change and hardly casting unless they see a mark of a fish. Don't be that angler. Instead, be the one that sees a good-looking line in the topographic chart, checks the temperature of the water on the screen, and tries out the spot.

When it comes to rigging your electronics, the same rules apply as they do to cameras. I like to keep my electronics as low-profile as possible, and if I can, even mount them onto a slide-track system or arm that allows me to look at the screen when I need to but move it completely out of the way the rest of the time. Most new sit-on-top fishing kayaks feature either a transducer scupper, which is an enlarged scupper hole that allows the transducer to fit and sit below the waterline, or a removable center pod. The center pod allows you to mount your electronics, such as a battery and transducer, in a through-hull pod system that is self-contained and easily removed for storing or transporting your kayak.

Another system that has taken off in popularity among kayak anglers are handheld fish finders, or chart systems that are merely an app on your smartphone. Out of all the electronics that I use, by far the most convenient and useful is my chart-plotting app on my phone. This not only lets me scout and chart the areas that I want to fish the next day, but it also lets me pull up maps of anywhere in the country rather than relying on a graphics card for a particular area, like you have to do for some fish finder charts. There are also new handheld fish finders that feature a floating transducer and either connect to a handheld monitor through a cable or connect to an app on your smartphone. These electronics don't require mounting or rigging to your kayak, so they are perfect for anglers who fish from inflatable boats or from multiple boats and need something that can transfer from boat to boat easily.

No matter how much you choose to rig up your kayak, you can always tweak your setup to make it more kayak fly-fishing specific. Stand in your kayak, like you'll be standing in it on the water, and look down at your feet. Imagine a circle with a diameter of 2 feet—that's the area where you want to focus your snag-proofing, as any and all fly line that gathers while stripping or casting will most likely land here and you want to remove anything it can snag on.

Grab a roll of high-vis tape (blue painter's tape works well) and mark any nuts, bolts, tab ends of straps, buckles, or anything you could image your line snagging on. Then with black marine tape (the black will prevent glare from the sun while you're on the water), cover everything you can. This will allow your line to easily slide off instead of getting tangled. After you think you've covered everything well enough, stand in your kayak again, but this time bring your fly rod. Send out a handful of casts, letting the line from your reel hang and dangle around the kayak's deck to make sure nothing is snagging.

Deck padding can be another handy addition to your kayak, especially if you plan on standing for hours on end while sight fishing, casting, or paddling. Look up the popular marine padding companies out there and find the one with the best kit for your exact model of kayak. The kayak-specific models are cut to size and will account for any hatches or scupper holes that are standard on your kayak. This padding may only be a few inches thick, but it will feel like a cloud compared to the hard plastic of your kayak's hull. The padding is also a nonskid layer for when waves cross over onto your boat, so you won't slip and fall into the drink.

SAFETY GEAR

The most important gear you can keep on your boat is the gear that will keep you alive and help you get back to the launch in one piece. Some gear is required by the Coast Guard, while other gear is just a good idea, or designed to make life a little easier on the water. Either way, make sure to bring these essentials along every time you're on the water and keep them within easy reach so that you can access them quickly in the event of an emergency. There's no use in bringing along safety gear if you can't even reach it.

The easiest first step to being safe on the water is something you should do every single time you hit the water and is as simple as putting on your lucky fishing hat: wearing a PFD, or personal flotation device. Wear a PFD often enough, and in the right model for you, and it eventually becomes a tool to help you catch more fish. The right PFD should fit you well and work with your body, not restricting it, and be comfortable enough that you will forget it once you start fishing. When trying it on in the paddle shop, make sure your arms can move unrestricted so that you'll be able to paddle and fish comfortably, without friction or rubbing. The PFD should also be able to be tightened properly, evenly all around, so that it will not ride up above your mouth, causing you to float with your mouth submerged should you fall in.

Required by the US Coast Guard (USCG) when fishing coastal waters, aboard your kayak you should also have a device to make

A kayak trailer can make unloading and loading your kayak much easier, meaning going fishing is more enjoyable.

Make sure to wear a PFD every time you hit the water, no matter what. A properly fitted PFD will not move at all when you're floating in the water, so make sure to adjust it snugly every time you put one on.

sound, such as a whistle or a horn. If fishing at night, you're also required to have a light visible from 360 degrees that is above your head and a visual signaling device, such as flares. Many kayak fishing gear companies sell a white 360-degree light attached to a pole, with a high-vis orange flag attached at the top, which is perfect for both day and night fishing.

You should also carry a first-aid kit, which will address any common accidents that you may encounter while fishing, such as cuts or lacerations, and in saltwater, a marine VHF radio. The radio is essential for calling in emergencies to the Coast Guard, communicating with bigger powerboaters driving by, or even communicating with friends who you are fishing with to find out where the fish are. It's a good idea to properly learn how to use your marine VHF before you hit the water, as accidently calling the Coast Guard isn't something they take lightly.

Other things that you should be carrying along are a change of dry clothes in a dry bag in case you accidentally fall in, materials to start a fire so you can properly warm up, and a rain jacket so you can stay dry should a storm sneak up on you. A few bottles of water and some high-calorie protein bars can come in handy if you've been out on the water for a long time and start to lose energy, or if you become stranded and need to spend the night. Carrying an extra paddle, even if you

Make sure your reel seat is properly tightened; otherwise, the reel might fall off while you're fighting a fish.

normally fish with a pedal-drive system or a motor, will make sure that you can always get back to shore should your primary paddle break or get lost while fighting a fish. There are many breakdown paddles available on the market, which can be packed away in a hatch until you need it and won't break the bank.

Safety Apparel

While all anglers should dress for the conditions, anglers fishing from a kayak are much more at the mercy of the elements and should dress in a way that will keep them safe on the water. Anglers fishing from a big center console could do so in a T-shirt and jeans, even though they shouldn't, and would likely be comfortable for the day, if a little sunburned. If kayak anglers fish in jeans and a T-shirt, they'd be soaking wet within minutes, shivering with cold soon after, and flat-out miserable, on top of being in a dangerous state.

The easiest way to think about what to wear before hitting the water is to dress for the water temperature, not the air temperature. Even if you're going to be fishing in 70-degree temperatures during a warm day in the spring, if the water temperatures are in the low 40s or even the low 50s, you're going to run the risk of hypothermia if you can't get out of the water and dried quickly enough.

If you're fishing in water that is cold enough to induce hypothermia if you were to flip and become wet, proper immersion gear is an absolute must. Even when fishing for warmwater species, there is still a good chance during periods of cold weather, or depending on the season, that an angler can run into water that is cold enough to call for immersion protection. A smart idea is to measure the temperature of the water with a stream thermometer, available at most fly shops, or with your fish finder's transducer. Make sure to dunk your transducer or thermometer deep enough into the water to measure the true temperature of the water, not just the top few inches near the surface where the warmer temps will throw off the gauge's reading. If the water is colder than 60 degrees Fahrenheit, wearing immersion protection is an absolute must, since you have a much higher chance of lowering your body temperature to dangerous levels. Even if the water is more than 60 degrees, there is a chance of hypothermia if it is windy or if you stay wet for a long period of time. If there's a chance that you could get wet, or if the river you are fishing is moving swiftly enough that you could make a mistake and fall in, wearing immersion protection is still probably a smart idea.

The best form of immersion protection is a dry suit, the best of which are made from breathable materials like GORE-TEX, which allow moisture from sweat to escape the confines of the suit while still keeping you dry. The dry suit usually does not feature any insulation elements, but allows you to layer clothing underneath so you can control your body temperature based on the conditions and wear the same suit all year long. A dry suit keeps water out by utilizing something called a gasket, usually made from latex, at the neck and wrists, which keeps all water from getting

Harry Duchesney ties on a yellow and white Clouser Minnow, the best fly for the striped bass in skinny water on Cape Cod. Notice the facemask and long-sleeved UPF 50+ shirt that he's wearing to protect himself from the harsh summer sun.

into the suit. Soft booties allow anglers to pair their dry suit with proper footwear, like wading boots or river sneakers, depending on the fishery in which they'll be spending the most time. Dry suits can also add a little fun to your day when you watch your friends try to put one on for the first time, as they're known for being a little tricky. The easiest way to put one on is to get a friend to help you zip it up, or consult your dry suit's instruction manual for more specific tips.

If you're fishing in water that is more than 60 degrees and don't think that immersion is likely, I recommend wearing breathable wicking materials, which will do more than just keep you comfortable. The best clothing to look for is a long-sleeved shirt and long pants that are lightweight enough to keep you cool in the sun but also feature UPF protection to protect you from the sun's harmful UV rays. It's like wearing clothing as sunblock, which can't be washed away throughout the day. A few newer clothing lines even feature high-tech fabrics, some antimicrobial or hydrophobic, maybe even both. Hydrophobic means that water will run off the material as if you were wearing the feathers of a duck. Antimicrobial material fights off bacteria buildup, which not only keeps your skin healthy all day long, but also inhibits the funk caused by sweating and catching fish, no matter how many days you're out there.

At the very least, stay away from materials that will weigh you down or make you cold when wet, like cotton or denim. Wearing jeans or cotton T-shirts is an easy way to get yourself in trouble on the water, as these materials will hold moisture and dampness for a long time, making you susceptible to hypothermia. Synthetic materials, or even natural ones that are still warm when wet, like wool, are a much smarter clothing option for paddlers looking to fly fish from their kayak. Besides, half the fun of getting into a new sport is looking the part, right? So why not look like you know what you're doing by investing in some kayak fly-fishing clothing that will keep you safer and more comfortable on the water?

I've mentioned it a few times already in this book, and I'm sure down the road you'll be reading more about it, but that's because I can't stress this point enough: Wear a PFD every time you go out in a kayak. I must stress this again and again because an alarming number of people out there don't bother with PFDs and get themselves in trouble, with deaths increasing every year as more and more people try fishing from a kayak. Even some of the readers of this book right now are probably thinking that they don't need to wear a PFD, but they'd be wrong. Yes, I'm talking to you. There are a couple arguments that I hear over and over again when people try to convince me that they don't need to wear a PFD. The first is "but I can swim." Sure, you may be able to swim like Michael Phelps in a controlled setting, but what if there's current, or the water is cold enough to take your breath away and put you in shock so that you're not thinking clearly? What happens if you get knocked out before falling into the water, or even when you're underwater, and your beautiful, technically perfect butterfly stroke is useless? A PFD is designed to save you *when* you can't, not *because* you can't. No one is going to think that you're incompetent if you wear one.

The second argument I hear, probably as much as the "but I can swim" excuse, is that PFDs are uncomfortable. First of all, death is pretty uncomfortable, so that's not a good enough excuse, if you ask me, but secondly, if a PFD is properly fitted to your body, you should forget that it's there altogether. With so many different sizes and designs available for every body shape and multitudes of materials to chose from, there's no way there isn't a PFD out there with your name on it. My recommendation is to go to a paddle shop, not a big department store with a clerk that has no idea what they're talking about, I mean a real paddle shop, and ask for help. A good shop will listen to your needs and help you find a PFD that's perfectly tailored to your style of fishing and paddling, as well as your body.

My favorite PFD is actually an inflatable one from Mustang Survival called the Elite. It's designed to contour to your body and is so lightweight that I've hopped in my truck and driven halfway home before I noticed that I was still wearing it, usually as I was walking into a store to grab a bite to eat. While inflatable PFDs aren't always the right choice for everyone, especially paddlers in moving water where getting wet is very likely, they are a smart choice for anglers who aren't comfortable wearing a full PFD for hours on end. If an inflatable PFD sounds right for you, I suggest finding one that automatically deploys once you hit the water. The one I wear, mentioned above, deploys if you go more than an inch or two underwater, meaning it deploys faster than you could even start thinking about pulling the ripcord. It also features a manual ripcord, in case you decide you need some inflation at any given moment.

One final accessory that you should pair with your clothing and PFD getup is a trustworthy PFD knife, or dive knife as it's sometimes called. If you're fishing in moving water this is an absolute must, as moving water increases the chances of falling in. The knife will help you cut loose if you become entangled with something underwater or maybe even something attached to your boat, like a gear lanyard. Even if you're not fishing moving water, a quick-release, blunt-tipped knife attached to your PFD will be a handy tool in everyday fishing scenarios, like trimming

Joe Gugino, cofounder of Why Knot Fishing, pulls his Hobie Mirage Outback out of the water after a cold day searching for landlocked salmon on the fly. Notice how many layers of waterproof material like neoprene that the angler is wearing to stay warm and dry.

line, rigging lures, or cutting bait. The blunt tip protects you from puncturing or cutting yourself in rough water or if you're not paying attention, and the quick-draw sheath lets you present your knife as soon as you need it. Practice drawing the knife from its sheath at home before heading out on the water to find the best mounting location. You should be able to draw the knife without even thinking about it or reaching awkwardly; everything should be done in one swift, fluid motion.

Paddles

The most common misconception of those new to kayak fly fishing is that a good paddle is a waste of money, so when a beginner is buying their first kayak, they just grab the cheapest paddle they see hanging in the paddle shop and hit the water. While this will get you around on the water and can help you catch plenty of fish, the difference between using a good paddle and one that is subpar is substantial. The paddle is your motor. Paddling with the cheapest paddle you can find is like driving around in a budget sedan that was a hand-me-down from an older sibling. Sure, it can get you around town, but it's not very fast, doesn't look very pretty, and isn't any fun to drive. The high-end paddle, on the other hand, shining beautifully in the shop window, likely made from carbon fiber or another lightweight material, is like a Ferrari. Not only is this paddle gorgeous and much faster than your basic paddle, but it's also a lot more fun to drive around, which is the most important part. Sure, you can get from Point A to Point B with a basic paddle, but that high-end paddle will be so smooth and so dreamy, slicing through the water and propelling you with minimal effort, weighing barely anything in your hands, that you'll genuinely enjoy paddling, no matter the distance.

Whenever anglers ask me which paddle to get, without fail my answer is "the best one you can possibly afford." While breaking the bank on a paddle that is worth more than your kayak can be extreme, the best paddle that you can afford will give you the most joy on the water and help you fall in love with kayak fishing from the get-go. If you're paddling with a cheap paddle, it's going to be heavier, require more effort per stroke, and won't get you as far on every stroke. When you feel like you can't get anywhere while kayak fishing, you'll want to jump into a big boat with a motor and forget about your little plastic boat. If your high-end paddle lets you cruise along with minimal effort and maximum speed, and you can focus on fly fishing from your kayak instead of huffing and puffing and straining yourself while paddling, you'll keep fishing from your plastic boat for years to come.

It's tough to really grasp the full effect of the quality in a paddle. When you first get into a fishing kayak, or any paddle craft for that matter, your technique is going to be all wrong and you're likely to be using all the wrong muscles. If you don't have the right technique, you're sure to wear yourself out faster and you'll think that paddling is too hard, no matter how good the paddle you bought felt in the shop. As much as I'd love for everyone to be able to go out and drop $500 on their first paddle, not only would that be financially irresponsible and likely catch you a lot of grief from your significant other, but you'd also miss out on the drastic step up in feel once you graduate to something better. For the first few months, try a midrange paddle. I'm in no way suggesting you get the super-cheapo paddle, because there's a point where it'll degrade the experience, but much like buying a bottle of wine, get the second price-bracket paddle, not the very cheapest. After paddling around with that cheap paddle for a while—maybe a month, maybe a few months, maybe even a year—try out a better paddle. If you go for a significant style upgrade, like fiberglass or (*shudder*) metal to a carbon fiber shaft, you'll immediately see the difference and buy the better blade on the spot. If you go for the same style but just better quality, like from a $200 paddle to a $400 one, you're only likely to notice a difference over the long term.

I saw this firsthand when I was on a trip with one of the pros in this book, Juan Veruete, whom you'll meet later in the warmwater rivers section. I had been paddling a fiberglass, high-angle, straight-shaft paddle for years, and he tossed me his paddle. Not only was it made from carbon fiber, but it also featured

Experiment with the feather angle of your paddle to find which fits best with your paddling style.

a low-angle blade, a bent shaft, and a price tag likely triple what mine cost. While I'm still not a huge fan of the bent shaft, even after paddling one on whitewater trips, the difference was staggering. Once I got over the awkwardness of the bent shaft in my hands, I was cruising in the current of the big river much more easily than with my old paddle. I tried to ignore the fact that Veruete was visibly struggling with my paddle while I enjoyed this hot rod of a blade and shaft combo, but after a little while I swapped with him. It was more out of pity than kindness, I'll be honest.

Going back to my paddle, the differences were too obvious to ignore any longer. The fiberglass felt as heavy as lead, and the high-angle blade felt like it was pushing back against the river's current with every paddle stroke. Something else that I realized after paddling Veruete's carbon fiber beauty was how badly mine flexed. A problem I would never have noticed before trying out his paddle, I could now see how much effort I was losing, just gone, with every single paddle stroke. My high-angle paddle blade may have been able to produce more power, but even with that advantage, our speeds were much closer than they should have been.

As soon as I got home from that trip, I went out and picked up a shiny new blade of my own. It may not be the same bent-shaft paddle as Veruete's, but it is made from better materials and it feels lighter in the hands than anything I've paddled before. Simply put, the better your paddle, the more enjoyable a day on the water can be—though it still helps if you catch a few fish while you're out there.

STRAIGHT SHAFT VS. BENT SHAFT

The right paddle for you depends on your body type and the style of paddling that is most comfortable for you. The shaft is the center of the paddle, the part that you hold in your hands. There are a few reasons why paddlers choose a bent shaft over a straight shaft and vice versa, but the easiest way to decide is to think about how much paddling you'll be doing at a time.

For paddlers who plan to spend long days on the water, paddling long distances, a bent shaft will be more comfortable all day long. This is because while using a bent-shaft paddle, your wrists are in a more comfortable position at the catch, or the start of your forward stroke, and will reduce the risk of a repetitive-use injury. For paddlers with a previous wrist injury, it's smart to start with a bent-shaft paddle. Bent shaft also has a disadvantage, though, since your wrist will not be at the best angle when paddling backwards, which is common when fishing tight against the bank or paddling in a river where you must frequently back ferry, or paddle backwards, to remain in position along the river. These paddles also make it more difficult to perform a stern rudder, or using your paddle as a rudder, placed at the stern, to steer your boat straight in current or waves, as well as harder to low brace, or using your paddle to push off of the surface of the water to remain upright. (See more about different paddle strokes in the following chapter.) Bent-shaft paddles also tend to be more expensive and are often slightly heavier, as more material is required to create a bent paddle shaft of equal strength to a straight shaft. Bent-shaft paddles are most common with long-distance paddlers like sea kayakers, or kayak fly anglers who are fishing offshore or covering a lot of miles in a day.

The most common paddles that you will see, and will find at any rental shop, are straight-shaft paddles. For most beginners, it is easier to learn proper technique with a straight shaft. While straight shafts are slightly less efficient for longer days on the water, plenty of anglers cover a lot of miles with them. If you're going to be fishing tight to the bank and need to frequently paddle backwards, it may make more sense for you to get a straight shaft. Straight-shaft paddles are lighter than bent shafts and are usually cheaper, which is why you see more of them. As a general rule, it's better to start with a straight shaft while you're learning to fly fish from a kayak, and then as you progress you can graduate to a bent shaft if your joints are sore after a long day or you're planning to spend more time on the water. If you're fishing a more technical river, or if you need to perform more advanced paddle strokes, a straight shaft will also make it easier to execute these maneuvers compared to a bent shaft.

HIGH ANGLE VS. LOW ANGLE

Another big decision when choosing your first kayak paddle is the angle of the paddle's blade, which describes the shape of the blade. Think of blade angle as power, as in how much power you want to produce from each stroke. With a high-angle blade, you're creating more power for faster paddle strokes or short bursts of speed compared to a low-angle blade, which is designed for lower power spread over more paddle strokes. It's the same as a car with really fast acceleration compared to a car that has cruise control and is in it for the longer haul.

When paddling with a low-angle paddle, your hands should never be raised above your shoulder, which allows you to comfortably cruise mile after mile on the water, without applying too much pressure to your muscles or your joints. The proper technique for a high-angle paddle is to allow your hands to go above your shoulders, up to your cheek or eyes, which allows your blade to apply the maximum amount of power against the water. Much like the bent shaft versus straight shaft debate, anglers who spend more time on the water paddling, covering longer distances, may want to have a low-angle paddle blade. For anglers in tighter environments, or in fast-moving rivers where you need to execute a move in the least amount of paddle strokes, a high-angle blade is more appropriate. Hunt down a local kayak demo day with your favorite paddling shop and ask to try each style of paddle, bent and straight, low angle and high angle, in different combinations, until you find the one that feels right.

PADDLE FEATURES

Many companies now offer paddles that have been designed specifically for the kayak angler and include handy features like a fish measuring ruler, usually running along the paddle's shaft, for quick measurements of fish before release, and hook retrievers built into

Instead of pulling through the paddle stroke with your hand close to the water, push with your opposite hand. Make sure your body stays centered in the boat so that you don't push yourself off-course.

the blade. These hook retrievers, which are usually a small shape cut out of the bottom of the paddle blade, are designed to remove hooks and lures from areas where you are snagged, like on a submerged log or in a tree. Don't laugh—when you're first learning to fly cast from a kayak, you're likely to catch your own tree pounder or giant stick fish.

Some companies have also started to include adjustable ferrule systems, so you can adjust either the length of your paddle or the feather angle of your paddle blades, or both. Fishing from a kayak often requires a different length of paddle for different scenarios. While sitting down, you want your paddle to be long enough to reach the water to submerge your paddle blade without reaching to one side and banging your paddle shaft on the gunwale of your boat. If your paddle is too long, you're likely to dip your paddle blade too far into the water, causing drag to build on your paddle shaft and your stroke to lose efficiency. If your paddle is too short, you're more likely to hit your kayak's gunwale, lose efficiency in your paddle stroke when your paddle blade cannot fully go underwater, and become injured by constantly reaching side to side in order to fully submerge your paddle blade. When standing, you'll want your paddle blade to be submerged the same amount as when sitting, so most anglers will hold one paddle blade with their top hand and use the paddle like a standup paddleboard paddle. If your paddle is not long enough, however, you'll be forced to constantly bend over at each paddle stroke, causing frustration and possible injury. An adjustable-length paddle will allow you to extend your paddle so it can be used while standing and sight casting, and then shorten it when you go to sit down and put in some miles.

When it comes to feather angle, each paddler has his or her own preference. I prefer no feather angle, which means that my paddle blades are exactly parallel, or to explain it another way, my paddle will lie flat on the ground. This is because the zero feather angle allows me to always know that I have the correct blade angle should I need to perform a recovery stroke, like a low brace, or perform a kayak roll when paddling whitewater. A few close friends, however, swear by a slightly offset feather angle, usually around 45 degrees, which allows them to retain a more neutral wrist angle—that is, their wrists are closely aligned with their forearms, producing a paddle stroke with less fatigue and less chance of repetition injury. Start with a feather angle of zero and watch your wrists. If your wrists are not in alignment with your forearms and you feel your wrists will become sore after a long day of paddling that way, experiment with feathering. You may need to feather your blade angle to 45 or even up to 60 degrees to keep your wrists neutral, or in alignment.

CHAPTER 3

Paddle Strokes

There are certain paddle strokes that kayak fly anglers will use more than any others, no matter where they fish. Some applications will require more finesse or technical paddle strokes, but if you know how to properly execute the forward stroke, sweep stroke, and draw stroke, you'll be able to set up your kayak for any situation that you'll encounter when fly fishing.

Forward Stroke

When I'm first explaining the forward stroke to new paddlers, they look at me like I'm explaining how to breathe. It's just paddling forward, right? Well, yes, but there's more to it than that. Just paddling forward without knowing the proper technique will surely get you across the water and to and from your favorite fishing spots, but you're likely to be more inefficient without proper technique, which will lead to fatigue, frustration, and possibly injury.

The proper forward stroke, and all paddle strokes that follow, starts with the setup. Hold your paddle with both hands, with your wrists in a neutral position, or aligned with your forearms and shoulders. This will prevent you from reaching side to side and causing injury, as long as you have a properly fitting paddle, as mentioned in the previous chapter. Your grip should be loose, but firm. Imagine you're shaking the hand of a person who you think

The draw stroke is an essential paddle stroke that will aid in positioning your boat along structure; just make sure not to affect your balance.

Paddling with proper technique will ensure you can stay on the water all day long, without fatigue.

is attractive—you want to apply enough pressure that they know you're confident, but not enough to overpower them. If you're holding onto the paddle with white knuckles or it feels like you're shaking the hand of a frat boy, trying to outmuscle each other, your grip is too tight. Your thumbs should be placed along the shaft, as if you're giving the thumbs-up with your hands sideways.

Once you have the proper grip on your paddle, start the forward stroke. The most important part of the stroke is the catch, or the start of the stroke when the paddle grabs or catches the water so that it can propel your boat forward. Keeping your arms comfortably bent and making sure that they stay in the same neutral position with your shoulders, rotate your torso to extend one paddle blade forward, up to your bow, or the front of your kayak. Insert the paddle blade into the water and instead of pulling with the strength in your arms, untwist your torso and use your opposite hand to push your other paddle blade forward through the air. This untwisting of your larger muscle groups is more efficient and more powerful than using your arms, which means that it is less tiring and makes it less likely to injure your smaller muscles. Imagine a line drawn across your paddle shaft, going up both of your arms and across your torso, at your shoulders. Think of this imaginary box as a real-life cardboard box that you cannot let fall. Keeping your arms and paddle shaft in this position, with this box in perfect form, will ensure that your paddle stroke is as efficient as possible.

If you're using a high-angle paddle, your top hand—the hand that pushes your paddle shaft forward, and is opposite to the hand with the paddle blade in the water—should be at the same height as your cheek or eyes. If you're using a low-angle paddle, this top hand should be at shoulder height, and no higher. When you've unwound your torso all the way, pull the paddle blade out of the water, in line with your hips. If you've properly kept the imaginary box in line, your paddle blade must come out of the water at your hips; otherwise, you will lose the box and lose efficiency with your paddle stroke. As you are taking the paddle blade out of the water at your hips, your other blade should be in the perfect spot at your bow, ready to catch the water and start the next stroke. If you keep this box in perfect form, your forward stroke should be in constant, steady motion, effortlessly pushing you across the water.

Sweep Stroke

One of my good friends, Juan Veruete, is a kayak fishing guide and instructor, bringing clients to the famed Susquehanna River in Pennsylvania and teaching them to catch giant smallmouth, even with a fly rod. He told me one of the easiest ways to find out if paddlers know how to sweep stroke is to ask them to turn their kayak around. Even those who are anglers first and paddlers a far second will appreciate learning the sweep stroke, as it makes life much easier. The sweep stroke is essential because there are many instances where an angler has nosed up to structure or the bank and must turn around quickly. Or, many times, especially when fishing in current, a paddler must be able to quickly spin the boat around with just one stroke. The anglers who Veruete instructs often have to use several strokes, sometimes more than ten, in order to spin their boat around, instead of using just one effective sweep stroke.

To start the sweep stroke, first you have to understand the difference between your paddle blade's power face and non-power face. The power face is the scooped side of the paddle blade that is strongest and most effective at pulling water. When conducting a forward stroke, the paddler should be looking at the power face, so that the paddle has the most effective surface to push against the water and

Make sure to pull your paddle blade up and out of the water before it hits your boat, or it will throw off your balance.

Properly exiting your paddle from the water will allow you to quickly reinsert the paddle blade for the next paddle stroke.

propel the boat forward. The non-power face is the other side of the paddle blade, and is less effective at pulling water.

When using a sweep stroke, start with the same catch, or start of the stroke, in the same position as the forward stroke. Instead of the paddle blade traveling along the boat's gunwale, or parallel to the gunwale, the blade should arc away from the boat towards the stern, or back of the boat. If your paddle blade were drawing a line in the sand, it would create a half circle that starts at your bow, or close to your bow, and ends at your stern, or close to your stern. Using the power

The draw stroke is a great stroke for aligning yourself in the wind or pulling up to a dock to get out of your boat at the end of the day.

Turning your blade at the end of the draw stroke will assist in pulling your blade up and out of the water before it hits your boat and throws you off balance.

face of your paddle to execute a sweep stroke will spin your boat most effectively.

There are many times when a reverse sweep stroke is more effective at spinning your boat. To perform a reverse sweep, just perform a sweep stroke in the opposite direction. Start by planting your paddle blade close to your stern, with your power face pointing forward, or towards your bow. Then, sweep your paddle blade out and away from your stern, in an arc towards the bow. This will spin your boat on the same side as your reverse sweep stroke rather than spinning your boat to the opposite side, like when performing a forward sweep stroke. If you're paddling in a river, the sweep or reverse sweep will be necessary to perform an eddy turn, which is spinning your boat into an eddy, the calm water behind a rock or obstruction in the current.

Draw Stroke

Many kayak fly anglers can fish season after season without knowing how to perform a draw stroke, but if only they knew its effectiveness, they'd use it every single time they hit the water. A proper draw stroke will allow you to slide your boat sideways without moving forward or backwards. Once I learned to properly perform a draw stroke, I instructed all of my friends and fishing buddies on the technique, and not a single day goes by when I don't perform a this stroke on the water, either to slide up to a dock or the bank to get out of my kayak more easily, to set my kayak closer to structure to keep fishing, or to stay inside an eddy when fishing or paddling in a river.

To properly execute a draw stroke, start by extending one paddle blade out and away from your boat, in line with your hip, and inserting the blade vertically in the water. The more vertical your paddle blade is in the water, the more effective the stroke will be, as well as more efficient. Continue the draw stroke by then pulling your paddle blade straight into your hip, turning the blade and pulling it out of the water before it reaches your boat, in order to keep it from colliding with your gunwale. Then set up the next stroke in the same position and repeat until you have finished sliding into the necessary position on the water. It helps to use your core muscles to power the stroke rather than using your arms. Imagine your core muscles pushing your hips and your boat towards the paddle blade, instead of using your arms to pull. This makes your paddle blade in the water an anchor, allowing you to more effectively power your stroke, using your larger muscle groups to move your boat sideways.

A slightly more advanced form of the draw stroke is called a sculling draw, which can be more effective for smoothly sliding up to a dock sideways or up to the bank. Instead of performing multiple draw strokes to slide your boat sideways, taking your paddle blade out of the water after every stroke, the sculling draw allows your paddle to remain in the water the entire time. Not only is this stroke easier when properly executed, it's also a quieter stroke and makes you look like an expert.

The start of a sculling draw is the same as a normal draw stroke, extending your paddle blade straight out and away from your boat, in line with your hip. Plant your blade vertically in the water and begin pulling the blade straight to your hip. Instead of bringing your paddle blade all the way to your hip, start to bring the blade towards your bow, then turn the blade's power face towards your stern and continue to draw. Repeat this back-and-forth motion from the bow to stern to bow, continually pulling your paddle blade towards your hip. Instead of your blade moving in a straight line from a point a few feet away from your boat straight into your hip, the blade instead moves back and forth, about half the distance to your boat. The sculling draw allows you to continuously slide your boat along, as long as you need to move sideways, without your paddle blade ever leaving the water's surface. When learning this stroke, it may be easier to perform a few back-and-forth sculling draw strokes, then remove your paddle blade from the water to reset into the proper position if the blade starts to creep too close to your boat, which is likely to happen when you're starting out.

Kayak Fly-Fishing Paddle Strokes

While seasoned paddlers will learn many more strokes over their lifetime, the forward, sweep, and draw strokes will get any angler across the water all day long, as efficiently as possible. There are a few other paddle strokes, however, that are specific to kayak fly fishing. Since so much of kayak fly fishing involves standing up in your kayak, either for sight fishing and finding fish or for ease in casting, paddling while standing up is an important skill. There are two ways to move your boat while standing, and some anglers choose to use either one or the other, or use whichever stroke is necessary in different scenarios.

The simplest way to paddle while standing up is to extend your paddle blade so you can paddle as you would while sitting down, or to slightly bend over, with your knees, to paddle normally. Bending over to paddle is effective only for small or quick position changes, as any extended bending over can cause fatigue or injury and is just not enjoyable.

The most effective way to paddle while standing up and sight fishing is to use your paddle like a standup paddleboard paddle. Slide your hands along your paddle shaft until your top hand is placed at the tip of your paddle blade and the bottom hand is placed near the center of the paddle shaft; you should be holding your paddle as vertically as possible. Most anglers prefer to use their non-dominant hand as their top hand, so that the bottom hand provides more effective control. For example, if you are right-handed, your left hand should be placed at the top of your paddle, holding the tip of your paddle blade, while your right hand is at the center, or near the center, of the paddle shaft.

Your forward stroke should start the same way as if you were sitting down, except your paddle should remain vertical throughout the catch and the follow-through. When you untwist your torso and your paddle blade in the water reaches your hips, twist your top hand, with your thumb pointing forward, so that the power face of your blade pushes out and away from your boat as you take it out of the water. This is called a J-stroke, if you can imagine the paddle blade's path creating the letter J in the water, and it keeps your boat from going in a circle when paddling on only one side. Many anglers choose to perform two or three J-strokes on one side before switching sides and performing the same number of strokes on the opposite side to keep the boat moving straight. It is possible to keep your paddle on the same side the entire time

Joe Gugino reels in a schoolie striped bass in Beverly, Massachusetts, during the midday bite, often the hardest time of the day to catch fish. Always be ready to switch from paddling to reeling in a fish, or you may throw off your balance and fall in.

Jennie Duchesney holds up her first striped bass ever, caught on a topwater popper on the flats of Cape Cod. Duchesney paddled into casting range before staking out her SUP and making a presentation to this fish.

you're standing up, which is my favorite way to paddle, as it saves time and allows you to pick up your fly rod faster should you spot a fish within casting range.

Another paddle stroke that can be very useful when kayak fly fishing is one-arm paddling. If one hand is holding the rod, hopefully fighting a fish, how are you supposed to position your boat so that you can land the fish? This often comes in handy when you're fishing in a river and want to stay in an eddy, fishing in the wind, or fishing close to structure. The easiest way to paddle with only one arm is to use your body as a fulcrum. Let's pretend you're holding your fly rod with your right hand. With your left hand, reach down the shaft of your paddle and place it where you would normally put your right hand when paddling. Now you can allow the left side of your body to act as the axis point and pull your left hand towards your bow, performing a reverse sweep, to spin your boat to the right. Many times you can use your elbow to keep the paddle close to your body, in this case using your left elbow in front of your paddle shaft and squeezing your arm as you perform the reverse sweep to allow your body to become the axis point. To spin your boat to the left, place your left hand in the same position you normally would and place the paddle shaft on the right side of your body. Allow the right side of your body to act as the axis point and push on your paddle shaft to perform a sweep. Make sure that the power face of your paddle is facing you, so that the sweep stroke is most effective.

Keeping your paddle in your lap while you fight a fish will make one-arm paddling easier and more effective, as you can immediately drop your paddle back into your lap after repositioning your kayak so that you can continue to battle or land the fish. You can perform a one-arm paddle stroke just as effectively while standing up, sometimes even more effectively, as you have your entire body to act as the axis point. Using your hips or your legs' quads as the fulcrum point will be most effective, and often you can improve the strength of the stroke by pushing out with your legs or hips to add more power to the stroke.

CHAPTER 4

Casting

Start fly casting from a kayak and you'll quickly learn the powers of adaptation. There are so many factors that will change the dynamics of your cast, like your kayak, your rod taper, your height, and even your seat height, not to mention the obvious factors like weather and target species.

I was fishing with Chris Funk, a kayak fishing photographer and owner of Feral One Photography, when I noticed just how deeply those adaptations weave into your fly-fishing psyche. Chris is an Alabama man and mostly fishes in rivers and swamps for his favorite species, shoal bass. That river fishing burned a hole in his style as much as my saltwater flats fishing burned into mine.

We were fishing a cove at Kentucky Lake for largemouth bass, and Chris set up within 10 feet from the bank. His big, open loops and short casts quickly got his flies within a foot of the bank and his topwater popper landed with a subtle splash. Sitting in his kayak, Chris drifted parallel to the bank, quickly picking off fish every few casts. While he worked the bank his way, my way was a different kind of beast. I angled my kayak nearly perpendicular to the bank, at least 50 feet into the lake. Standing up and looking for signs of fish and only then sending out a cast, my sidearm loops were, according to Chris, "tighter than a camel's ass." My fly landing softly into the water and leading the fish by a foot, I leaned forward as I stripped, crouching like a cage fighter.

It's easy to cast sitting down in your kayak once you learn to use the balance point of your boat to your advantage. Just be sure to find the balance point of your kayak before learning to cast while sitting down.

Author Ben Duchesney sends out a cast with a yellow and white Clouser Minnow near the North Shore of Massachusetts for a cruising striped bass. His casting style has developed over the years to be more sidearm so he can get under the wind on the saltwater flats. JON LEAVITT

Why would two anglers fishing for the same species, even using the same fly, execute it so differently? Because we've both adapted to the fisheries we fish most. My sidearm, tight-looped casting is bred from battling winds on the expansive flats. I have to stand up in order to spot fish, and casting before I see a fish is futile. Chris, on the other hand, has to sit down while river fishing; otherwise, he'd flip on every rock the current pushed him into. Using that current to send him downriver, he needs his casts to be short and frequent so he can hit a spot once, maybe twice, before he gets pushed past it.

Casting from a kayak is tricky at first, but once you get it down, you'll be able to concentrate on the things you love most. Instead of concentrating on not hitting the water on every backcast, you'll be able to enjoy the sunrise, feel the sun on your face, and land your fly on the nose of your next dream catch.

Basic Kayak Cast

Whether you sit or stand to cast in your kayak, the way you lay out line will be different than if you were wading or standing on the bow of a powerboat. One great thing about learning to fly cast well in a kayak is that it makes you more versatile in other situations. Being able to shoot 60 feet of line while standing on the seat of your kayak in light chop means you can bomb casts across the river when your feet are securely planted on the river bottom while wading. Think of learning to cast from a kayak as the advanced placement class of fly casting. You'll soon be on your way to Trophy Fish University.

Before hitting the water, hit the lawn. Casting in your yard is a great way to learn the mechanics of the kayak fly cast before you even touch water. Practice enough and you'll gain muscle memory, so doing it on the water will be even easier.

Find a beach chair, one that is low enough to almost feel the grass with your behind, and put it in the center of your lawn. Start with 10 to 15 feet of line, enough to load your rod quickly. Make sure your rod tip is close to the ground, as this will ensure your rod loads efficiently, which is crucial to the rest of the cast. On the backcast, keeping your rod near vertical above your shoulder ensures you have enough room above the ground's surface. Rather than at your side, like when casting while standing, your rod hand should be raised higher. Depending on your kayak's seat height compared to the water, you may need to have your reel at about the same level as your forehead. In kayaks with higher, raised seats, the rod hand can be lower, like at the ear.

Keeping a straight wrist at the top of the cast will ensure your backcast will not hit the water. Overextending the wrist or the arm on the backcast is a common mistake while fly casting from a kayak, as many think reaching back farther will keep the line higher. To make sure your backcast remains in the air, load the rod until the leader is about to come off the water and then snap your arm to a stop. Stopping the wrist abruptly will ensure that once you snap back the line, the line will unfurl evenly.

Once the rod's vibrations from the backcast dissipate, you can begin your forward cast. Leading with the elbow, snap the rod grip forward by pressing forward with your thumb and pulling back with your bottom fingers, the ring finger and pinkie. As the great casting instructor Joan Wulff says, the motion is similar to opening the button of a screen door, pressing the button with your thumb and pulling the door open with your pinkie and ring finger. Stop the rod when your thumb is pointing towards your target. Putting a target in front of you on the lawn, like a hula hoop or hat, will give you something to focus on and improve accuracy.

Once you develop muscle memory while casting from this seated position, try casting without the chair, seated directly on the grass. When even that doesn't faze you, try casting while seated in your kayak on calm, safe water. The key to maintaining your balance throughout the cast is to make sure your head stays in the center of your kayak—that way

Casting while sitting down requires careful attention to technique and casting form. Using your line hand (the left hand in this case) will allow you to double-haul, thus increasing your line speed, making it easier to cast while sitting down.

your center of gravity will remain in the same position. As a general rule, your body will follow your head when seated in a kayak. That means if you look over the side, down into the water, you have a much greater chance of going over the side, into the water, and taking an even closer look than you intended.

More Kayak Casts

One of the best basic casts to learn is the roll cast. Once you've mastered roll casting while standing, it will become your new best friend when casting from a kayak. Because you're already so close to the water, roll casting from a kayak is even easier, as your rod has more surface tension to load with.

To begin your roll cast in the kayak, start with your line extended out in front of you. It helps to send out a normal cast before roll casting. Raise your rod tip just beyond vertical to create what's called a D-loop. Your rod and line should look like the letter D, with your rod being the vertical spine and your line the half circle, which should be formed at your side or slightly behind your seat. The surface tension of your line in the water is what gives this cast its power. As your rod tip reaches the top of the D, snap the rod forward with the same stroke as your forward cast in the basic cast detailed above.

Your line should unfold in front of you and lay out flat, just like a basic cast. This is a great cast to use when your back is up against an obstacle, like trees or bushes. It is also a great cast for quickly getting your fly to a nearby fish right after you've casted to the wrong spot, or if the fish is on the move.

Double-hauling is a great way to ensure your cast remains in your control while seated in a kayak. A properly executed double haul will load your rod faster and increase line speed, which makes your loops tighter. A tighter loop is easier to keep off the water's surface on your backcast, as it gives you more breathing room.

The basic mechanics of the double haul are simple: Your line hand, the one not holding the rod, helps increase the load on your rod, on both the backcast and forward cast. As you raise your rod tip to load the rod, hold onto the excess line with your line hand. As you snap the rod tip back to begin your backcast, pull down with your line hand to load the rod faster.

As your backcast unfolds behind you, feed the line with your line hand into the backcast. This also helps set you up for the haul on the forward cast. Once the rod's vibrations dissipate from the backcast, pull down on the excess line in your line hand and snap the rod forward. When shooting line, simply let go of the line with your line hand and the excess line with be pulled into the cast, with a fast-enough line speed.

Line Management

The absolute toughest part of learning to fly fish from a kayak is not the cast itself, or paddling correctly, or even catching fish—it's line management. Not only is it difficult, but if you don't address the problem at the start and

Joe Gugino, cofounder of Why Knot Fishing, demonstrates a proper backcast on a small freshwater pond in Massachusetts. Now that the line has unfolded behind him, the next step is to begin the forward cast.

learn to do it correctly, poor line management can drive you crazy on the water and likely prevent you from catching any fish at all.

The first step in making sure your line is under control is setting up your kayak with line management in mind. Before your kayak even touches the water, set the boat out on your lawn, or somewhere you can cast without hitting something around you, and stand inside it. Make sure everything you plan to use on the water is also in your boat, including rod holders, fish finders or nets, and tools. If you're going to be fishing from a sit-inside or a type of kayak you won't be standing in, sit down. Strip out some line and make a few casts, then strip out some line and make a few more casts and repeat until you've cast all the way out to your limit. The whole time note any moment your line gets snagged on a piece of rigging or gear in your boat. Repeat the same process again and watch where your line falls at your feet or on your waist.

After noting where your line is gathering on the deck of your kayak, take some blue painter's tape and mark off the area. Then, measure 2 feet around that area and mark that off as well. This larger area is the zone where your line is likely going to grab onto anything that it can. Testing this before you start mounting will give you a better start at line management. If you've already installed gear within this area, move the accessories to

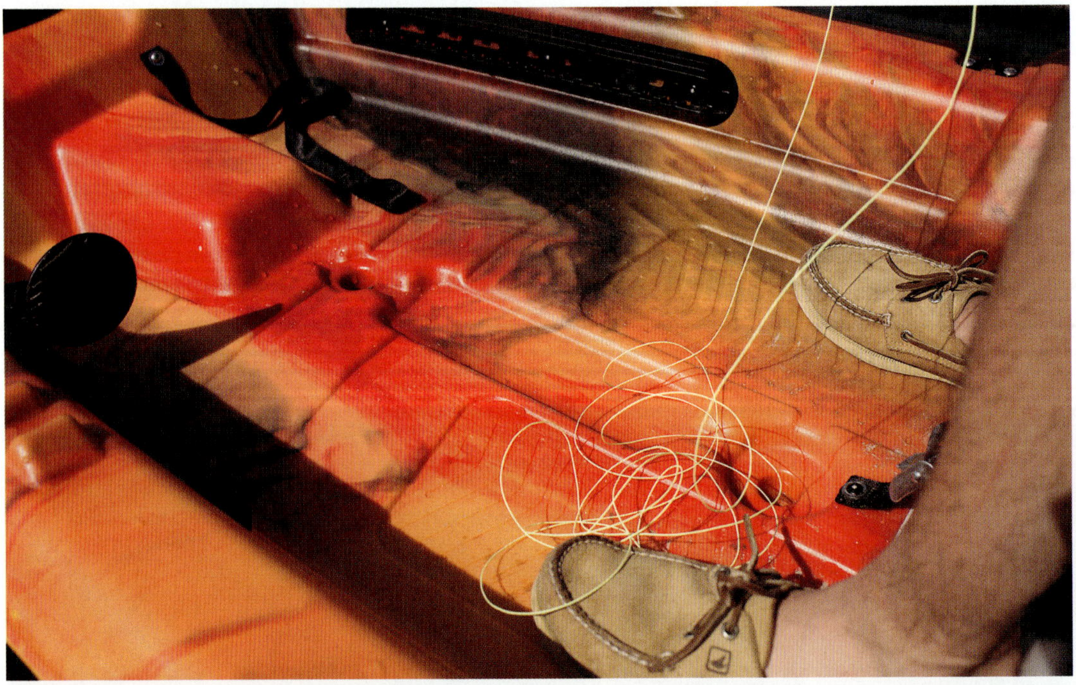

A kayak with a large, clear deck will prevent your fly line from snagging on every cast. Fly fishing in a kayak means you're going to snag your line often, but being aware of it will lessen the chance of a messed-up cast.

Kayak fishing guide Juan Veruete sends out a cast on his home waters, Pennsylvania's Juniata River. Veruete made sure his line wasn't going to get snagged so that his cast could unfold properly in front of him. JUAN VERUETE

a different spot if possible. If that requires removing screws, instead of leaving holes in your kayak, either mount accessory pad-eyes, available at any major marine outfitter, or put the screws back in after taking off the accessory. Make sure to add a dab of silicone sealant to each screw before drilling them back in to keep your kayak watertight. If you absolutely can't move your accessories, use electrical tape to cover any points where your line keeps snagging and pay attention when casting out on the water.

The point that most snags occur is right at the worst time: when you're shooting line. This happens because immediately before you shoot your line, when you've let go with your line hand and the line is sent out towards the fish or water, there is a tendency to exaggerate the motions of the cast. This extra effort, which is not needed and actually hinders the dynamics of the cast, makes the line coiled at your feet or in your lap move outside of the pile it has fallen into and causes it to grab anything nearby. Not only is this frustrating, but it can also be embarrassing, because it usually leads to a poor cast that spooks the fish you're casting to. This is easily prevented, however, by maintaining proper form throughout the entire cast, all the way to the follow-through when the fly lands in the water. If you've repeatedly snagged on something and have already moved everything out of the way and checked your form, grab a T-shirt or a stripping bucket and place it where the line can fall into it and not become snagged.

Snags can also occur when stripping, which is another awful time to happen, as it can hinder your setting the hook or fighting a fish that has just hit your fly. After checking the rigging on your kayak to make sure nothing snags, make a long cast (without a hook tied on the end of your line) and start stripping in line the same way you'd retrieve a fly on the water. If you're a striper fisherman, pretend there is a striper chasing your fly and use short, excited bursts of speed in your retrieve. If you're fishing for finicky trout and plan to slowly entice fish on a streamer worked along the bottom, strip with long, slow pulls with your line hand. Pay attention to where your line is gathering. Some anglers prefer their line collect at their feet into an area they've designated and prepared, while others prefer to strip line off the side of their kayak where it can collect on the water's surface, right beside their boat. Either technique works for different reasons, but stripping into your kayak is more cautious, as you know what to expect. When you're stripping out over the water, you run the risk of your line finding a single twig, rock, or powerful current, which will pull on the line during your cast and alter your line speed, distance, and worst of all, accuracy.

Think about where you'll be fishing and make sure to practice stripping in line both before you hit the water and when you start fishing. If you'll be fishing a small, quiet pond where there is little risk of snagging a rock or twig with your coiled line, it's less important where your line goes as you strip. If you're fishing bigger water or fast-moving rivers, you may want to keep your line inside your boat where you can keep tabs on it.

PART 2

Hitting the Water

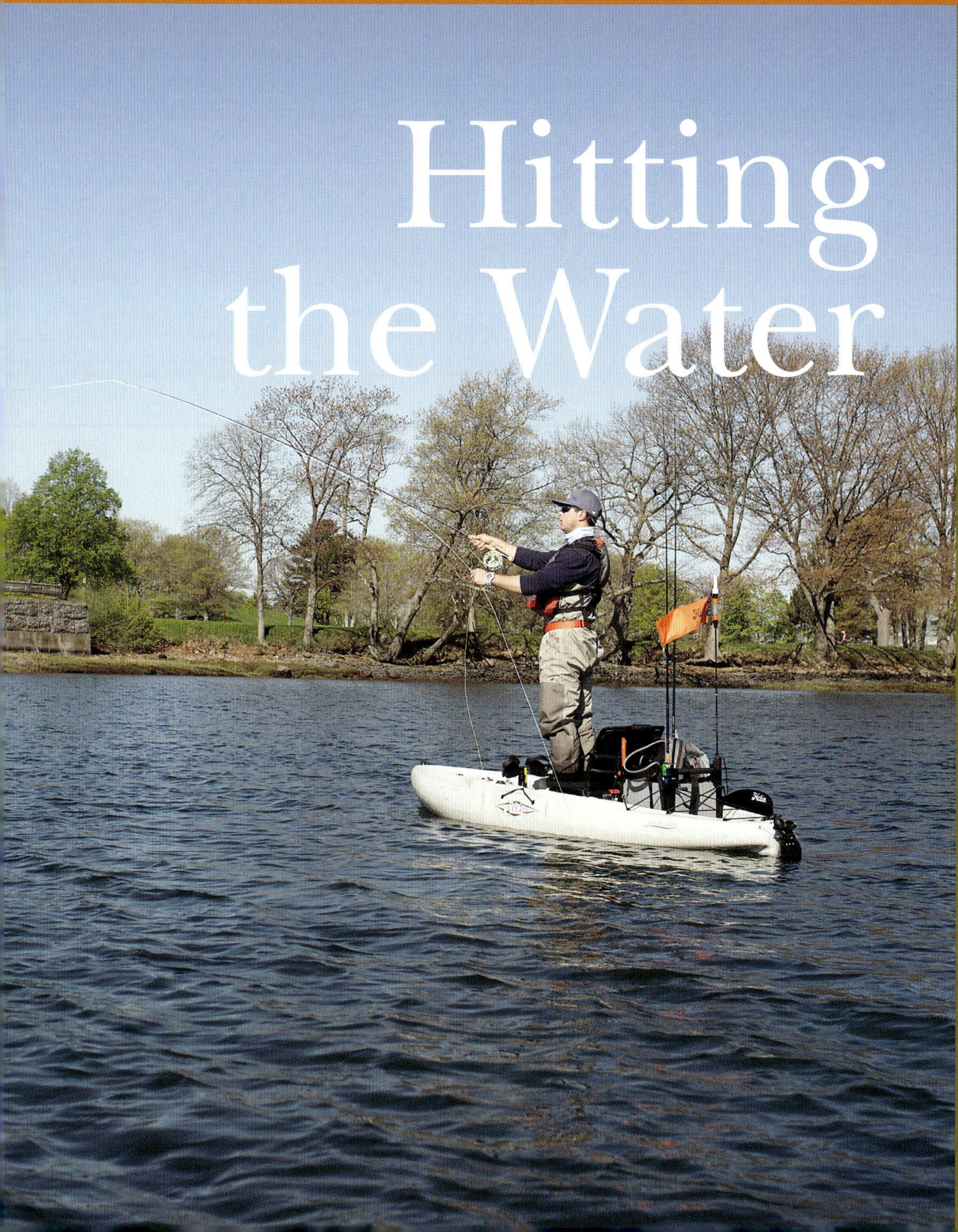

CarpPro

CHAPTER 5

Warmwater

The kayak fishing explosion really started in two places, right around the same time. The first was out in Southern California with kayak fishing pioneers Dennis Spike and Jon Shein chasing big-game species in saltwater. The other was in Florida in the ponds full of lily pads and giant largemouth bass with angler Ken Daubert.

"At four I was sneaking away to go bass fishing," says Daubert, who got his start like the rest of us: with a pocket full of worms, standing on a drainage pipe fishing for bluegill with a hand line. After moving to Florida in 1982, Daubert started guiding on saltwater from a skiff. "One day I saw a kid with a kayak paddle across thick weeds," he says. "It looked so easy." From then on he guided less and kayak fished more. Pretty soon he became known around the country as one of the original pioneers of kayak fishing, penning his own book, *Kayak Fishing: The Revolution*, and inventing his own lure, the Bass FROG.

Daubert fishes from a kayak for the same reason many other anglers choose to fish from these little plastic boats. "I like shallow water," he says. "Seeing the fish first, and then casting; the surface fishing. That's why the kayak, it has that stealth factor."

That closeness to the water and to the fish was the same reason I started kayak fishing. I originally bought the kayak to head out into the saltwater after big striped bass that I couldn't reach from shore, but I soon started hitting the many freshwater ponds near my home and quickly became addicted.

Professional fly tier Pat Cohen shows off the face of a big Mohawk River carp—a face only a mother, or an angler, could love.

Wood and structure along the water may be holding fish—make sure to throw a few casts alongside it before floating closer. This is the type of water that you can't target without a kayak to get you there.

That stealth factor that Ken Daubert grew to love is the same tactic I use on a daily basis every time I'm fishing for largemouth bass, smallmouth bass, or northern pike from my kayak. Pairing the stealth of a kayak with the precision and natural presentation of a fly rod brought me over the edge and I've never looked back. Now every time I fish, whether close to home or on a trip, saltwater or fresh, I bring a fly rod.

Fishing for warmwater species is less high-adrenaline, less intense, than fly fishing from a kayak in saltwater, at least in general. Of course, there are times and circumstances when freshwater fishing is an all-out melee of action, but the atmosphere is much more relaxed when there are no tides and currents to consider and weather seems to roll in much slower, and there is generally less boat traffic or competing anglers to worry about.

While some anglers focus all of their efforts on warmwater species and will plan full dawn-to-dusk days around them, I think they can also be the perfect fishery to hit for a quick trip before or after work or for introducing an angler to kayak fly fishing. With smaller fish (generally) and with less to think about, anglers cutting their teeth on kayak fly-fishing tactics and skills will have a much easier and more enjoyable time during the learning process—which means they're more likely to love it after they become experts.

The thrills in warmwater fly fishing come in bursts separated by long, quiet moments. I once was fishing in upstate New York on a slow-moving warm river looking for big musky on the fly, just down the street from where a previous world record fish was caught. We had been lazily paddling upstream, casting gigantic flies towards structure and looking for signs of moving fish. The heat combined with staring into the murky, tannic-stained water had me fishing seemingly half asleep as cast after cast came up empty. When the first musky swirled on my fly, I nearly dropped the rod in surprise and panic, totally ruining any chance at actually hooking up. For reference, the swirl of a musky on your fly looks and sounds like a cannonball dive from a water buffalo. Revitalized and shaking, I cast towards the next log with extra focus. A smaller musky, though still a 30-inch fish, burst from underneath the wood and halted just inches from my fly, staring right into my eyes, through my soul. Before I had a chance to twitch the fly once more and get him to strike, the musky ghosted into the deeper, darker water and we never saw another fish that day. There's no going back from an encounter with a big fish like that, and it's hard to find that in any other form of fishing.

Pond Hopping

There's no other fishery that lends itself so perfectly to kayak fly fishing than small ponds full of eager fish. A lightweight kayak that you can throw over your shoulder with one hand while carrying the rest of your gear in the other makes it possible to jump from pond to pond in seconds, which is something no other boat could do.

This is where I perfected my skills at kayak fly fishing, as Cape Cod, where I was born and raised, contains 365 lakes and ponds cut and shaped by the glaciers receding from the last ice age. When I look for a new pond that's ideal for a lightweight run-and-gun pond-hopping mission, I look for water that I can cover in a single day. Larger lakes that take more than one day to cover every inch of water will fish much differently, as the fish will orient themselves on different structure and points than they would in smaller bodies of water. A pond is even better if access is tougher or requires hiking in, since nobody but a kayak angler would be back there.

The great thing about smaller ponds is that you can cover the entire pond in a day, so choosing where to start is less important because you'll get to it all eventually. Regardless of that fact, though, I usually always try to put in on the downwind end of the pond, for

In the early summer you can cruise the shallows targeting bass that are holding on their beds. Letting the wind push you along shallows like this is the best way to target the whole area without spooking fish.

two reasons. The first is because after a long day of kayak fishing, I'll likely be tired and want the wind to carry me all the way back to the launch. Try doing that in a big, heavy boat.

The second and much more important reason is that wind tends to congregate bait, whether that's shad or other kinds of baitfish under the water's surface or bugs scattered on the surface. Fish follow the bait, so anglers looking to hook up should also follow the bait. Fishing the downwind side first either will let you start hooking up right away and begin to pattern what the fish are keyed in on or willing to bite, or will let you cross off that part of the pond first and move on to the next.

If the downwind side is not producing fish, which tends to happen when the water is colder, like in the spring, it may be because the fish are stacked up in the warmer waters of the upwind edges of the pond. This is where the most effective tactic for pond hopping comes into play: beating the bank. Not only is beating the bank an extremely effective tactic for catching fish around the spawn, or before the dog days of summer, but it can also be the most exciting way to fish. Pulling your fly through a shallow sand flat along the drop-off of a pond and watching a big bass come out of nowhere and slam it is truly unforgettable. I tend to circle the entire pond, casting to nearly any enticing structure or pattern that is within casting range. Besides drop-offs or edges leading into varying depths of the pond, fish may be locked onto structure, such as stumps, rocks, or downed trees, where they can hide and wait to ambush prey. In order to catch more fish, you have to imagine that your fly is the prey and then put it in the spot where it will most likely be ambushed.

The great thing about fly fishing from a kayak when beating the bank is that you can orient your position better and easier than someone in a bigger boat, or especially an angler wading on shore, ever could. If you've chosen a kayak that allows you to stand up, you'll have the best vantage point for searching for edges and structure in the water, as well as spotting fish. Even if you can't stand up in your kayak, the fact that you can rotate and maneuver the boat with the flick of your paddle means you can make a cast much sooner than an angler waiting to spin his big johnboat with a slow trolling motor.

Wind will constantly be a factor when fly fishing from a kayak, not just because it may affect your cast, but also because it will spin and move your boat much more drastically than if you were fishing from a bigger boat. If you're fishing with a wind pushing your boat along the bank too quickly, there are two techniques to slow yourself down. You can either point your kayak into the wind, which will reduce the boat's profile, thus giving the wind less surface area to push against, or you can use a drift sock. Since pointing your bow or stern into the wind tends to be only a temporary solution, or a solution for lighter winds, keeping a drift sock in your boat is a great idea. Essentially a drift sock is a small parachute that you attach to one end or side of your kayak and let drift behind you in the water. The open parachute will grab the water and create more drag, making it harder for the wind to push you along the water's surface. If you don't have a drift sock handy, many collapsible mesh nets will work, though not as well and efficiently.

While you're fishing, your paddle should rest in a dedicated paddle holder or in your lap, right at your hip, which will keep the paddle out of the way but also accessible at the same time. If you're fishing in windy conditions and must constantly correct your boat's position between every cast, it makes more sense to leave it in your lap. If there is no wind or you like the speed at which the wind is blowing you, keeping the paddle out of the way in a dedicated paddle holder means you can really focus on fishing.

Controlling your boat while fighting a fish is where kayak fishing separates the pros from the rookies. Controlling a boat with one hand

Sparse fly patterns will consistently fish better than flies that are overdressed. In fly tying, less is more. The weight makes the fly a little more difficult to cast, especially in wind, but it's worth it when you hook up.

while fighting a fish with the other shows how much more skilled we really are compared to our big-boat brethren. If you've decided to store your paddle in a paddle holder, make sure it's in a position that is easily reached with one hand. If you have to use two hands to retrieve your paddle, it will be useless during a fight with a good fish.

Whether the paddle is in your lap or in a paddle holder, controlling your boat while fighting a fish comes down to the same concept: leverage. With only one hand to paddle, you must rely on your body, specifically your waist. Your kayak's gunwales can also assist in making sure your paddle shaft is at the proper angle to the water, using that as sort of a secondary axis. Imagine your fly rod in your right hand, a good bend in the rod and all your slack line put onto your reel. The fish is running and is trying to drag your kayak right into a downed tree, causing you to lose the fight. With your left hand, pick up your paddle from where it is sitting on your lap, near your hip. Your left hand should be in the same position along the paddle shaft that it would be for completing a normal forward stroke.

Where your right hand would normally go, place that point along the shaft against the front of your right hip. Use your hip as the axis point as you push off with your left hand, causing the paddle blade on your right side to push against the water, spinning your bow to the right and moving the boat backwards. You can either continue to spin your boat in this manner and drift in front of the downed tree, or execute another stroke on your left side to move straight backwards.

To perform that same paddle stroke on the same side that you're holding the paddle shaft on, slide your left hand up to where you would normally put your right hand for a forward stroke. This stroke is much more awkward and tricky than just paddling with one hand. Once your left hand is where you would normally put your right hand on the forward stroke, place the paddle shaft where your left hand would normally go on your left hip. Pull back on the paddle shaft and your hip will act as an axis for the shaft to rotate; your bow will be pulled towards the left and the boat will continue to move backwards.

If you're standing and must use your paddle to maneuver your boat, your chest becomes that leverage point. There is some

Standing up to cast can increase your chances of spotting cruising fish in the shallows. Make sure to keep your fly rod close by when paddling standing up so you can switch back to fishing at a moment's notice.

disagreement among anglers as to whether it is more difficult to paddle with one hand while sitting down or while standing up. I think it's easier to get your paddle blade in the correct position while sitting down, but if you are standing up you have a trick up your sleeve for adding more power to your stroke that you don't have sitting down (more on that in a second).

Picture the center of your chest, right at the sternum, that leverage point or axis on which your paddle must rotate. The angle of your paddle shaft will be much steeper when standing up, with the top paddle blade next to your head and the other in the water next to your kayak. If your fly rod is still in your right hand, for example, your left hand must hold the paddle at the tip of the paddle blade instead of the paddle shaft. This will give you much more leverage when executing the stroke itself.

In the same motion as if you were sitting down, pull back on the paddle blade with your left hand; the blade on your right side will push against the water and move your boat backwards. That extra power I mentioned earlier can come in handy if you're fishing in current or in heavier winds and need to power your boat through some chop. As your paddle blade in the water starts to lose power, you can extend your knee towards the bow of your boat and create a secondary fulcrum point for your paddle shaft to rotate on. Driving the paddle shaft forward with your shin, just below the knee, can push your boat backwards even faster and ensure you're in control of your boat, even if you have to paddle one-handed.

PRO TIPS FOR FISHING SMALL PONDS AND LAKES

I like fishing with experts in their field. The more you fish with someone much better than you, the more you learn and learn fast. When it comes to fishing for bass and other warm-water species with a fly rod from a kayak, the most exciting way to fish is with a big, bushy bass bug, which is a fly that features more fur and feathers than you could imagine fitting on a single hook. Most bass bugs are designed with a buoyant head, usually made from deer hair or foam, followed by a tail and body made to add flash and movement to the fly. The combination of these materials creates a fly that rides on the surface of the water at rest, yet on the retrieve the fly will dart under the surface and shake or wiggle with a pulsating action that warmwater species simply can't resist. The king of creating and tying these bass bugs and warmwater patterns is a tier named Pat Cohen.

I've had the privilege of fishing with Cohen a few times, the first time being when I met him in the back parking lot of a U-Haul dealership somewhere in upstate New York after driving four hours before the sun rose. Giant beard, gauges in his ears, and tattoos covering his body, I could tell he was my kind of fishing partner.

Putting in below a dam among a flock of bird-watchers, who were staring at us with annoyance and confusion, we paddled across the current into a cove of calm water, looking for carp. After paddling around for a bit not seeing a single fish, we hiked up to the top of a nearby cliff and scouted for signs of carp.

Pockmarks littered the bottom, like chicken pox on a first-grader, signaling that carp were in the area. Near the opposite shore we could see a few big shadows moving through the water and we rushed back to our kayaks. While I couldn't convince a carp to bite that day, Cohen hooked, fought, and landed a giant 20-plus-pound carp on one of his own creations, the CarpNado, a buggy pattern that has convinced carp from all over the country to bite, even though they are probably the pickiest eaters in freshwater.

Before he starts choosing his fly pattern du jour, though, Cohen likes to do a little research on the new waters that he's going to fish, especially if it's a small pond off the beaten path. After finding a choice-looking body of water on Google Earth or through word of mouth, he might even do a little scouting before he brings a fly rod, especially since some waters are too small to discern details on satellite images. "I try to do whatever homework I can at home from the computer, whether that's Google Earth or a local Fish & Wildlife site," he says. "Even on some of the forums, every once in a while you can catch a name of a small body of water that someone went on, something only the locals will know about."

The next thing Cohen looks for is the structure, the key to discovering where the fish will be, and what kind of presentation will work best that day. "I'll ask if there are weed lines, lily pads, areas of cattails, a little island of grass in the middle, or maybe fallen trees," he says. Even the color of the water can be a hint as to the forage in the water, or what to expect from a new body of water that you might not have seen in your research. "I look at the color of the water to see how tannic it might be," he says. "A lot of the small bodies of water around me tend to be swampy, kind of like flooded forests, so they tend to be really tannic, which tells me right away that the oxygen levels might be lower, which means the fish might not be as big."

Signs like water clarity can start to paint the picture of your fly choice, especially when you have no other clues from your research to go on. One thing that helps an angler choose the right fly is knowing the local forage of a particular region, even in general terms. "I know in my area what the general forage is going to be for pretty much any body of water that I'm going to hit," Cohen says. "I'll go prepared for various kinds of baitfish and crayfish, or it could be a mouse pattern if I'm fishing topwater, and I try to bring some kind of insect, maybe a dragonfly nymph or damselfly nymph. When I go out on the water, I carry everything with me, including the kitchen sink. I try to go prepared for everything."

On top of that, Cohen also likes to bring a few patterns that imitate smaller largemouth bass. "Largemouth are cannibalistic—they'll eat other largemouth all day long," he says. Other baitfish patterns that work well in Cohen's area of upstate New York and anywhere around the Northeast region of the United States are perch, golden or silver shiners, and bream species like bluegill. Before you try to make a random guess as to the forage the fish are feeding on during a particular weather pattern or season, approach

Fishing for big musky requires giant flies. Here kayak fly-fishing guide Brian Cadoret holds up two flies tied by professional tier Pat Cohen in a pattern he has named the ManBearPig.

the water with the idea of scouting the forage first, before you look for fish. "Lets say I get out on the water and I find a school of baitfish," says Cohen. "I don't know what it is initially, but I see that they're in the 4- to 5-inch range." Pick a streamer—Cohen says the color doesn't matter much as long as it's the same size as what is present in the water—and make a few casts. "I'll make ten or twelve casts with that, and if I don't get a reaction or a follow or anything, I'll stay in that same size range because I know that's what's there, but I'll switch colors," he says. If you've tried four or five colors without a strike or reaction, it's time to switch. "I say OK, maybe they're not eating this, maybe that was just that particular school of baitfish that was there," says Cohen. When it comes to picking the next size of fly, he says to go for one extreme or the other. "I'll either go really big and try to get a

Professional fly tier and Jackson Kayak pro staffer Pat Cohen lands a cast at the base of a big tree and hangs on for a strike from a big musky in Vermont.

reaction bite, or I'll go much smaller and just see what I can find," he says. "From there a pattern starts to form, and eventually I'll start to know what these fish are targeting in on."

When you're throwing big baitfish patterns or bass bugs, all of which will likely feature terrible air resistance and make it harder to cast, Cohen likes to use a bigger fly rod than other freshwater anglers. "Most of the time I have an 8-weight and a 9-weight with me in the kayak, and I like to have them set up and ready to go," he says. "And I have two different flies on each rod." The bigger weight sizes of rod allow Cohen to throw bigger patterns, yet still retain enough touch and feel to detect more-subtle bites in tougher conditions. When rigging up the two different rods, he likes to vary his line styles to make sure he can present flies differently and make his fishing setup more efficient. "I'll have a floating line on one and a sinking or intermediate line on the other, but that also depends on the situation and the day, and the flies I'm fishing," he says. Even though Cohen fishes waters that are full of big, toothy fish like northern pike, he still uses monofilament leaders rather than a steel leader that a dedicated pike angler would tie on. "If I'm bass fishing with a sinking line, I'll just go with a straight 3-foot piece of 20-pound Berkeley Trilene monofilament," he says, "usually with no taper at all." When he switches to a floating line, he may use a slight taper.

No matter which leader style Cohen chooses, he likes to make his own leaders from different lengths and styles of line—that way his presentation is exactly how he needs it to catch fish in small ponds. "I make them myself and just blood knot my sections together," he says. "I usually start out with a pretty stiff butt section, because a lot of my topwater flies are pretty big so I like to be able to flip them over." Keep in mind a ratio that keeps 60 percent of your leader as a heavier butt section, followed by one or two sections of thinner-diameter line leading up to your fly. Cohen says his DIY leaders are perfect for chasing all of his favorite warmwater species, except carp. "When I'm carp fishing, I need them to be 9 feet long, and I want them to be really smooth," he says. Since carp live in waters with lots of weeds and they can be extremely finicky, making your own leaders can present a problem. "Unless you're covering your blood knots with something like Knot Sense from Loon Outdoors, blood knots catch weeds, and when you're carp fishing, catching weeds sucks."

Having two fly rods that are rigged up and ready to cast also allows Cohen to use his secret weapon when targeting warmwater fish. He likes to call it the "comeback cast." "A lot of the time these fish will follow, follow, follow, but there's no commitment to a fly," he says. "I like to have a second rod at all times so that if I get a fish that won't commit but is real hot, like following the fly around but not eating it, I can grab that other rod immediately and cast another fly out there that's significantly different from the first fly." Casting out a secondary fly that's completely different from the first will often trigger a reaction from the fish, as it won't suspect the comeback presentation. If you get a strike on the comeback cast, hang on, as they can be

A box of flies and some liquid fuel are two sure signs of a successful day on the water searching for big musky in upstate Vermont. Having a wide array of fly patterns to choose from will let you adapt to the conditions as the day progresses.

the most violent strikes of the day. "I store rods in the holders that are built into the sides of my Kilroy," Cohen says. "The active rod that I'm fishing with stays in between my feet, lying on the bow, while the one rigged for the comeback cast will be in the rod holder on my right, ready to grab."

While Cohen is picky about where he puts his rods, he doesn't put too much added effort into rigging his boat for his style of fishing. "I really keep my rigging down to a minimum," he says. "I like to keep the boat free and clear of obstacles or anything that can tangle up my fly line." The only customizing he has done to his boat is placing a PanFish Portrait camera mount and Dog Bone combo from YakAttack, set up with a GoPro, near the bow. "Other than that, it's pretty basic," he says. "I use a Vedavoo boat bag to store all of my fly gear, and that stays up near the bow of the boat for easy access." Cohen says to keep it simple, as the more things that you stick on the boat, the more likely you are to catch your line and tangle up.

Among all the different types of anglers, fly anglers have a reputation for being snobby or elitist, which is something that Cohen says will cost you fish if you're not careful. "Fly fishermen can be stuck on themselves and overlook things like bait fishermen," he says. Cohen says a bait fishermen you might normally walk right past can be the best research or key on any body of water, whether you've fished there before or not. "Here's the difference—most fly anglers I know are catch-and-release, which means we're out there for sport," he says. "Bait fishermen are not out there for sport. Nine times out of ten, they're out there for a meal, which means they're not screwing around, they're not hunting for fish. They know where the fish are, and they also know what the fish are eating. A lot of people would benefit on the water if they stopped and said, 'Hey, how's it going, how's the fishing going today, what are you using, are you catching anything?'" Cohen says that quick conversation with an angler on the bank can give you a better starting point than hoping to spot the right school of baitfish as you're paddling out to your first spot.

Cohen has another warning for fly anglers, who can get stuck in their own heads day after day. "We get stuck in a rut as anglers and we do the same thing over and over again, working the same water, working the same water the same way," he says. When it comes to smaller ponds, changing tactics and being sensitive to the changing conditions are paramount to hooking up. "Some of these smaller bodies of water, maybe they see a lot of people, or maybe the fish are well fed and you need to try to get a reaction out of them," Cohen says. "I find a lot of people, because they think they know everything about that water, they're afraid to change tactics." If he is stripping a fly in really fast but it's not yielding any results, he will change tactics, even though that speed may have worked the day before. "I always say that I've never fished the same water twice, because things are constantly changing," he says. "Barometric pressure changes, maybe it rained, maybe something new was introduced to the system, maybe the water temperature changed, maybe there was a hatch—you never know. If you're not constantly changing what you're doing and trying to evolve, and trying new tactics on the water, you're never going to catch fish consistently."

If there's one thing Cohen wishes anglers would learn more about when it comes to fly fishing, it's the science of how fishing works, not how to fish. "Everyone knows that smallmouth bass eat crayfish, but most anglers don't know how that all works, like what size to use at different times of the year, how often they molt, the fact that when that water hits 50 degrees there's a brief window in the spring when adult crayfish become available to smallmouth for the first time," he says. "The biology of crayfish, as it relates to bass fishing, that's the stuff that I like to know—it makes you a better angler." Time

Cohen admires a 25-pounder caught on a fly of his own creation, the CarpNado.

to start dusting off your old marine biology books from high school.

Cohen has used that better understanding of biology to develop fly pattern after successful fly pattern designed to catch big warmwater species all around the world. With creative patterns and even more creative names like ManBearPig, Stank Leg Slider, and One-Eyed Willy Popper, he has created a name for himself and for his company, Super Fly, as one of the most innovative in the industry. Since that first time fishing with him, I've been impressed by the action of his flies and his ability to pick apart warmwater fisheries and develop a pattern. We spent hour after hour fishing a lake in Vermont recently, trying for a last-chance bass after a morning spent getting skunked on a nearby river for northern pike. Of all three anglers, Cohen was the only one that day who hooked up, even

Wetting your knots before tightening them will make the knots tighter and hold better than a dry knot.

though we were fishing in super-clear water under bluebird skies in the middle of the day, normally very tough conditions. Tying on a big, flashy deer hair popper, Cohen started picking apart the weed lines until he got the first and only strike of the day. Though his 8-weight fly rod barely bent against the weight of the tiny largemouth bass, sometimes you have to take what you can get.

Warmwater Lakes and Reservoirs

The question I always get when putting in at a bigger lake or reservoir with my kayak and a fly rod in hand is, "How are you supposed to cover the whole lake with that thing?" The secret is, you're not.

The great thing about fishing with a fly rod from these little plastic boats is that it makes you slow down and focus on each spot, even each cast, much more than the average angler normally would. I recently paddled up to a fairly large cover in my local lake, a lake that would take me a few days to even just paddle and probably a week or two to fish the whole thing, at the same time a bass boat motored in. After maybe five casts without any luck, the bass boater fired up his outboard and threw up a giant wake that made me want to yell out after him. Since he had the luxury of testing out a bunch of different spots in a day, realistically with the entire lake at his disposal, he could throw a few casts into every corner and find the easiest fish in the pond. For the angler that isn't interested in catching only the lowest common denominator fish, like me, fly fishing from a kayak is probably more your style. That's why I ended the day with a worn-out arm from catching so many fish in that one cover that the bass boater just couldn't handle sticking around in for more than a few casts. Forcing yourself to slow down and focus on fewer spots means you have the luxury of truly fishing that one spot more thoroughly, with more precision, than any other form of fishing. You don't have to go far to catch lots of fish when you're fly fishing from a kayak.

When looking at the entire lake and trying to decide where to put in, I use the same thought process as when fishing smaller ponds. The downwind side has a greater

The crystal-clear waters surrounding Beaver Island, Michigan, can make an angler feel like he's paddling in the Bahamas looking for bonefish, not for big, 20-pound carp.

chance of holding bait and therefore holding fish, but it can also bring me back to the take-out after a long day of fishing if I've paddled into the wind. Hopping from cove to cove is basically the bread-and-butter of fishing in a kayak on larger bodies of water. Since we don't have the range of a big powerboat, we need to be able to pick apart water more efficiently than other boaters.

When approaching a cove, I initially look for any obvious structure or drop-offs that I should hit first. If there's nothing glaringly obvious at first glance, I'll likely check my GPS chart on my fish finder/GPS unit. This way I can make sure that I'm hitting the most likely targets first and then working my way around the rest of the water. Look for drop-offs, edges, or points extending into deeper water that sit directly adjacent to shallow water. Fish will most likely be cruising these lines and ambush points, waiting for bait and forage to be caught by surprise. You can take advantage of their hunting instinct by giving them an easy target, your well-presented fly. If there is obvious structure, though, like weed lines, vegetation, stumps protruding above the water's surface, or downed trees, fish will likely be orienting themselves close to that structure—again, looking to ambush their prey.

Depending on the time of year and the water temperature, fish may be closer to or farther away from the structure. If the water is cold or it is near the spawn, fish will likely be holding very close to the structure, so making sure your casts land as close to the structure as possible is a good idea. It's also smart to start farther away from the structure with your first few casts and then work your way in, just in case outliers are patrolling the edges of the structure. This way you have a better chance at catching more fish from within the same piece of water and same piece of structure, rather than catching one fish at the deepest spot in the structure and spooking every other fish around when you set the hook.

If there is no obvious structure at all, or obvious points on the GPS map that are presenting a good ambush point, I will likely work the cove the exact same way I would fish a smaller pond when pond hopping. Start at one end of the cove and beat the bank all the way around until you reach the other side. If you start catching fish, pay attention to where they were in relation to the bank, what depth they were holding at, and how you retrieved your fly. The only difference between decent anglers and great ones is paying special attention to what they are doing when they catch a fish so that they can replicate it exactly over and over again to keep catching fish.

If you've completed your bank-beating around the entire cove without a bite or sign of life, start moving into the deeper water, where the cove begins to meet the rest of the lake's deeper water, and look for fish that are likely suspending or orienting themselves to deeper structure that you won't be able to see, except for on your fish finder when you're directly above it. Many anglers fishing from larger boats or boats with motors don't have the luxury of hitting this secondary water after they've beaten the entire bank because their boat creates more draft and has a much more significant presence than a kayak. The added stealth of fishing from a kayak means that you can float directly above the fish while fishing the bank and then after only a few minutes' rest, go back and fish that same water you just floated over. It's a good idea when hitting this secondary water to start at the same end of the cove that you started at while beating the bank. This will give the fish more time to forget you were ever there before trying to catch them again. If you still haven't caught fish while hopping from cove to cove and systematically picking them apart, it may be time for plan B.

When coves and inlets fail, it's time to look at the last resort but still very effective tactic for the kayak fly angler: trolling. Not only can trolling with a fly rod allow you to cover a lot more water than casting, but it is also one of the deadliest ways to present a fly in front of many more fish. Since a fly is much more realistic and effective than the average lure, keeping your fly at the exact depth the fish are holding at gives you a greater chance at hooking up with fish than your buddies throwing giant crankbaits or jerkbaits.

When choosing a rod that's better at trolling than casting, a slower-action rod will allow you to present the fly much more subtly and will give you a better chance to set the hook before the fish even knows that it's hooked. For trolling I tend to choose flies that will pulsate in the water and give off as much action as possible. Flies that are made of bucktail present a great shad imitation, but the most effective material that I like to throw is bunny strips. Strips of bunny will give your well-trolled fly the feeling of coming alive and will impart a much more erratic action than any lure, which fish won't be able to resist.

A sturdy rod holder that is positioned in a place on your kayak's deck that still allows you to paddle efficiently means you can maintain the perfect speed and fish at the same time. Mounting the fish finder within reach but also in front of you as you paddle means you can carefully watch the rod tip for a strike and never miss a fish. If you do see a fish strike, paddle a few more strokes extra hard and you're likely to set the hook without even touching the rod, doubling your chances of landing the fish. Octopus or circle hooks are another smart idea when trolling, and most flies tied on these hooks will work just as well while casting. Another tip, try to choose hooks without barbs, as it makes it easier to release fish unharmed.

While it is possible to troll a fly rod without electronics, a fish finder and GPS combo unit will make your day more productive by leaps and bounds, allowing you to focus on areas that are more likely to produce. When looking at your GPS unit, there are a few areas to focus your trolling efforts. Depending on the time of year and the water temperature, fish could be holding anywhere from 5 to 25 feet, so choosing a path that samples different water depths is a smart idea. Even when deciding a route along a certain depth, it's a good idea to zigzag as you're paddling to vary your depth a little, and to also add pauses in your trolling retrieve to entice even more fish.

Once you've found the depth fish are holding at, either by catching fish or spotting them on your fish finder, focus your efforts

Chris LeMessurier paddles quietly through the crystal-clear waters of Beaver Island, Michigan, trying not to spook the big, 20-pound carp.

within a few varying feet on either side of that depth. The most productive areas of a lake for trolling are the saddle between two islands or higher spots on the lake bottom, where the bottom will dip between the two high spots, as well as along edges, drop-offs, or underwater structure. Zoom out on your GPS chart and look for high points that extend out into deeper water in a peninsula. You're looking for areas where fish could be waiting in the deeper water to ambush baitfish and smaller prey that are coming from the shallower water.

PRO TIPS FOR FISHING BIGGER LAKES AND RESERVOIRS

Much like the coldwater fisheries that we'll discuss in the next chapter, big lakes and reservoirs can be seriously tough to pick apart and develop a pattern. One of the most frustrating trips that I have taken in my career as a fishing writer was to a little island in the middle of Lake Michigan. Beaver Island is known far and wide as a haven for fly fishing for carp, as the gin-clear waters that surround the tiny spit of land can make an angler feel like he's in the Bahamas, not the Great Lakes. Sure enough, as soon as we hit the water in our kayaks, it looked like a postcard from the Caribbean, complete with colorful houses on the shore and giant fish swimming in the shallows. Those fish, of course, were giant carp.

My co-angler for the trip was Kayak Fish the Great Lakes founder and Michigan native Chris LeMessurier. LeMessurier spends nearly the entire year fishing these inland oceans for fish that would make your knees weak, everything from trophy smallmouth and largemouth bass to behemoth king salmon. I thought having a Midwest native show me around Beaver Island would give me just the right amount of fishing mojo needed to hook up with the most stuck-up and skittish fish I've ever encountered. Carp are also known as the golden ghost or poor man's bonefish, so I knew going into the trip, a three-day weekend of fishing from sunrise to sunset, was going to be long and especially frustrating. What I didn't know was that it'd also be one of the few trips of the year that I was skunked on—or at least almost skunked.

Instead of fishing the entire lake from a kayak, which would have been entirely useless without days of research, planning, and scouting, LeMessurier and I focused on the coves and points that we could target and pick apart more effectively in one long weekend. It didn't help that neither he nor I had never fished for carp at that point and had literally no clue as to how to catch one. Tying on the buggiest, bushiest nymph patterns we could find in our tackle boxes, we each tried our own version of flats fishing that we were used to, LeMessurier with a background in fishing Lake St. Clair for smallmouth bass, and me fishing the white sand flats of Cape Cod for striped bass. In case you didn't know, bass and striper tactics do not work on carp—at all. Refusal after refusal sent us both screaming and cursing into the heavy winds that would crop up in the early morning. Instead of leaving our flies completely motionless and letting the carp investigate them on their own time, and then deciding to eat, we would twitch,

Chris LeMessurier holds up a big trout caught on one of his home lakes. Proper research is what allows him to catch big trophies like this. CHRIS LEMESSURIER

skitter, strip, or pulse our flies constantly, trying to entice a bite. If carp were as aggressive as bass and stripers, that would have been one of the coolest trips of my life, like something out of a fishing movie. Luckily, though, there was a backup plan that made sure we ended every day with our hands smelling like fish, not shame.

Had LeMessurier been fishing a new lake system back home, not on a spur-of-the-moment trip with me, he would have spent a few days dissecting the water and gathering intel to decide where to launch and how to fish the lake. "When you're dissecting a new lake to fish in a kayak, you have to be more efficient," he says. "You can't just run across the lake to fish one spot and if it sucks run all the way back, 5 miles across the lake." Being able to dissect that water and break it into smaller, more manageable chunks also helps when you're casting with a fly rod. LeMessurier says, "You have to be efficient on how you use your energy when you're casting—you don't want to be making pointless, inefficient casts." He puts most of his thought on where he suspects the fish will be orienting on the new lake—that way when he launches his kayak he can launch close to where the fish will be, maximizing his time actually fishing, not paddling around. "Focus on structure and what the pattern might be," he says, "then position yourself as best as possible. You have to be more specific about where you put in compared to fishing from a motorboat."

When you've picked the right spot to launch and can get on the fish faster, your whole day becomes easier. Not only is it easier to find fish, but it's also easier to start developing the pattern, which LeMessurier says is the most important step to catching fish on a big lake. "You take the big picture and then you step it down," he says. "You think about the seasonal pattern: What are the fish doing? Is it a spawning thing, pre-spawn thing, or post-spawn thing? Is it a summer thing? Then you break it down again to their feeding habits and how they're going to be looking for forage, and then again down to what specifically those fish are going to want."

Choosing a fly based on this principle is less about *what* fly and more about *what kind of* fly you're going to be throwing. Instead of saying I want this fly or that fly, you're thinking about this style of fly or that one. "Ask yourself, are fish likely to chase their forage right now or should I pick a fly that can be fished still?" says LeMessurier. No matter how confident an angler is in the fly choice, no matter what, it's all a guess. "You aren't a fish, you can't read their minds, you can't ask them, so you're taking a guess at it, but its an experiment," he says. "Listen to the fish and let them tell you what's working and what's not working, and readjust." If you find that fish are refusing your fly or having a negative reaction to it, it's time to change. What that change is depends on the reaction, but LeMessurier says it could be something like, "Maybe it's a smaller fly, maybe it's a color change. Be conscious of what you're throwing and what you're doing so you can tell what fish are reacting to and know what needs to change first."

If you're not sure where to start fishing first or where to put in your kayak, LeMessurier says to look where structure changes. "I like bass and pike, fish that I can get a lot of action on, so I like casting and stripping versus drifting or slow-sinking presentations," he says. "I look for structure that those type of fish are going to focus on, like rocks and weeds." Since he prefers shallow water, he's also looking for depth changes, especially those that coincide with structure changes. "I'm either in lily pads/weeds type of structure combined with shallow water to deep-water or deep water with big drop-offs," he says. "The weeds that provide ambush points on those drop-offs, that's what I'm looking for. A weed line on a drop-off from 2 feet to 10 feet, that's where I feel I have the best shots at fish."

Positioning yourself along that structure change is important so you don't spook fish that are cruising around and looking for bait.

Chris LeMessurier releases a giant rainbow trout caught in one of the back pockets of his home lake. Without a heavier rod and reel combo, he would have lost this fish in seconds. CHRIS LEMESSURIER

"Close but not too close," LeMessurier says. "That weed line, for example, I like to be upwind of it, on anchor, but using an anchor trolley to position my boat either parallel or perpendicular to the wind." He says that positioning your boat properly can help with making sure your presentation is up to par. If the bow is pointed at the structure, for example, "I can stand up and get a much better cast versus trying to make a cast in a sitting position," he says. If the wind is a little stronger and standing up isn't a good option, LeMessurier will position his boat perpendicular to the wind using the anchor trolley and will sit sidesaddle, dangling his legs in the water. "That way I'm in a semi-sitting position," he says. "You can really extend your back and arms, so I can use better technique that way than sitting in the chair with my knees bent." That sidesaddle position will also aid in line management, usually the trickiest part about fly fishing from a kayak. "Then all of my line is in my lap or in the water where my knees are and it's a much cleaner way to have your stripped line or slack line kind of sitting in front of you," he says.

Since LeMessurier spends most of his time chasing bass and pike, fish that both require different tools to chase them, he wants a rod and line combination that is versatile over precise. "Typically that's a 5- to 7-weight," he says, "and I prefer a sink tip because I tend to do more streamers and moving baits, like crayfish patterns, which require a strip retrieve." The sinking line allows LeMessurier to work his flies a little bit faster, since they sink faster. Though he fishes topwater occasionally, with frog or hopper patterns on floating line, he says a sinking line is the more versatile of the two. "If it's not sinking, it's not doing much. You have to wait, and I'm not a patient person," he says. "That sink tip lets me strip it up a little quicker and let it sink back down faster; it works that water column a little better. Especially when working a streamer, that sinking line makes the presentation more consistent, since I don't have to wait for it to recover and sink back into position in the water column before I strip again."

It's that consistency that many bass and pike anglers rely on to fool fish into striking. A bass or pike will track a baitfish's movement and, like a quarterback leading a receiver, plan its striking route accordingly in order to intercept its prey. As for line style, LeMessurier wants that sinking line to be weight-forward—that way he can throw those bigger, hairy streamers that big bass and pike love to hit. When it comes to bass and pike, he falls into the camp that believes the fish are "too dumb to care" about leaders. That means he's not using the stealthiest choice of leader because he doesn't have to; instead, he goes for strength. "Most of the time I'm running a fluorocarbon leader, probably 7 to 9 feet long, and probably in the 8-pound up to 12-pound strength range," he says. "Sometimes I'll tie 12 or 16 inches of steel tippet onto my leader, just to make it more cut-resistant for the pike."

Even though LeMessurier spends a lot of time on the water, he doesn't believe in dropping serious money on a fly rod when there are many rods available at a much cheaper price that will still do the job. "I like a moderate to fast, something forgiving," he says. "I don't have a real pure cast, so I want something a little more forgiving." Rods in the $100 to $120 range are his favorite, he says, "something smooth enough that I can cast pretty far and is inexpensive in the world of fly rods. There are a lot of really good rods for really good prices." LeMessurier cautions would-be fly anglers to stay away from the budget combinations, though, so don't go looking in the bargain bin for the cheapest rod you can find. Instead, look for the best rod for the best price. "I don't believe in cheap—I think you have to have some quality to it," he says. Above all, try casting the rod before you buy it, or at least inspect the components and overall quality to make sure you're not spending money on a cheap rod that will break quickly, especially on a big fish.

A kayak fly fisherman sends out a cast in the fading afternoon light in the late fall, searching for landlocked salmon. Freshwater fish are often more static in their holding patterns, making them easier to find throughout the season.

While saltwater anglers will swear by a big reel, LeMessurier and many other freshwater anglers think of reels as mostly a line holder. "A large-arbor but inexpensive reel is a good choice, because for most of the fishing I'm doing, I'm retrieving them on the strip," he says. "Every once in a while I'll get them on the reel and fight them that way, but I'm not getting into anything that's taking me into my backing like a musky, a big trout, or saltwater gamefish." For carp, though, a good reel is a better choice, since you're fishing with leaders that are a little finer and stealthier. A good drag system will keep those lighter leaders intact while still letting you put a lot of pressure on the fish, meaning you might actually have a chance at landing it.

"Less is more . . . I know it's cliché, but I have very few accessories on my kayak when I'm setting up for fly fishing," says LeMessurier. "This approach allows me to keep a snag-free surface and be more productive when casting, fighting, and landing fish." His garage is full of kayaks, rods, reels, and rigging projects, as he's a conventional angler as often as a fly angler, but his kayak crate is the center of all his rigging customizations. "My customized milk crate is an invaluable piece of equipment on my kayak and has been perfected over the past ten years," he says. "Much more than a box to hold stuff, my crate helps me organize tackle, camera equipment, safety equipment, and much more."

As for LeMessurier's rod storage strategy, it's all about avoiding snags on the backcast. "I keep extra rods taken apart, in their cases, stored inside the kayak hull," he says. "I keep just one rod 'at the ready' and that simply lies on my lap while I'm padding." For fly storage, he looks for fly boxes that are big enough to hold giant, fluffy streamers—the bigger the better. "To be honest, I have yet to find a fly box that is too big," he says. "When that's not in use, I store it behind me in the crate." Most importantly, LeMessurier stresses being mindful when rigging your kayak—that way you won't waste time setting things up that you won't use on the water or won't help you catch more fish. "Be mindful of what you have on and around your deck/cockpit," he says. "If you simplify your approach, there will be less opportunity for problems and you will be able to focus on the fly fishing itself."

Every time our game plan on the flats of Beaver Island failed, LeMessurier and I would pack all of our gear back into my truck, hit the dusty dirt roads of the island, and drive into its center. At the heart of the island was a cluster of smaller ponds that were full of largemouth bass and northern pike. Tying on a spinnerbait triggered bite after bite, starting with our very first casts, which let us rest easy each night, smelling like fish. Having that backup plan allowed us to be more experimental with our tactics on the flats fishing for carp, which, even though it didn't end up getting us any fish, did allow me to learn more than I've ever learned on a single trip. Knowing that you can catch fish later lets you put more focus and effort into your plan A, which without the right knowledge and a few tips from pros who actually know more about the fish you're targeting, might not be a very good plan.

Warmwater Rivers

Some of the most productive days of my entire life have been fishing warmwater rivers. Since the spots where fish are holding can be more predictable than when fishing ponds or lakes, hooking up with a fish is just a matter of finding the right mixture of water flow and structure. Regardless of the species, fish—and really all animals—look for the same thing: the most calories for the least amount of work. If a fish can get a big mouthful of food by moving as little as possible, it has a greater chance at survival, because the number of calories it's gathered is greater than the number of calories it's burned that day. Anglers can take advantage of this when fishing rivers, whether for coldwater species or warmwater, by targeting the most likely spots that fish can find food without moving around too much.

A precaution you should take before putting in on your local river is what guides and whitewater paddlers call "rigging to flip." This philosophy reasons that there's a good chance you will eventually flip your boat, and will most likely flip it without any warning or time to hold down your gear, so you should tie down or attach lanyards to any gear that doesn't float. While anglers can get carried away with tying down their gear, strapping everything down to the point that it is getting in their way of paddling, fishing, or worse, getting back into their boat after they've flipped, you should still tie down the gear that will be costly to lose or won't float. Many gear lanyards on the market attach via quick-release clips to your boat and gear and are designed to break away or quickly detach in the case of an emergency. These gear lanyards will also allow you to use your gear as freely as if there were no lanyard attached, as they are usually designed to be stretchy or made from bungee material and will move with you. If you're looking to spend as little money as possible, though, you can rig up your own gear lanyards by visiting a local hardware store and finding either paracord, a thin, strong rope rated for high strength tolerances, or thin bungee that you can then tie to your gear and your kayak.

Now that you're safe to hit the water and prepared for all the challenges that fishing moving water can present, it's time to find the fish. Understanding how water flows around objects in the river will help you determine where fish will likely be hiding and where to place your cast.

When water is flowing downriver and meets a rock, the water has no place to go but around it. If the rock is deep enough in the river and surrounded by water on all sides, the water will flow all around the rock except for directly behind it. Imagine walking through a city on a windy day. If you hide behind a bus, you'll find yourself in a wind-free zone, surrounded by the wind moving around the bus. Water flowing downriver acts in the same way, unable to push water on the downstream side of the rock, creating a pocket of neutral water. These are also called eddies when the rock is large enough or breaks the surface of the water. You can easily identify an eddy in the center of a river by looking for a triangle of swirling water extending out from a rock at the water's surface and moving downstream.

Kayak fishing guide Juan Veruete sends out a cast on a warmwater river in Pennsylvania in search of smallmouth bass. He keeps his kayak crate secured with bungees and always wears his PFD should the river surprise him and make him flip his kayak. JUAN VERUETE

Not only do eddies provide a safe harbor for your boat to rest in the current without the need to paddle to maintain your position, but they also create a safe harbor for fish. Since fish survive by expending as little energy as possible, they will wait along the seams of the eddy and watch for forage to pass by in the current. These seams are usually the most productive places to cast your fly when river fishing, as the fish will be watching those exact spots. It's also possible that the bigger fish will be directly behind the rock, as deep into the slack water as they can possibly swim, so placing a few casts around the slack water gives you a good chance to hook up.

When fishing in rivers, locating and targeting these seams and eddies will usually reap the greatest number of fish. These current seams will often yield fish regardless of the fly you choose, though the most exciting is by far a topwater popper or slider pattern, especially for warmwater species. If the water is too cold and the fish are too lethargic to chase bait on the surface, these topwater flies are going to lose their potency. When this happens, a weighted streamer will allow you to probe the deeper eddies where fish will be hiding out and waiting for the warmer weather. If fish are still not reacting to your fly, or reacting negatively, downsizing your fly and switching to something with a more natural presentation will increase your chances of hooking up. As a last resort, switching to a subtle wet fly pattern can fool even the toughest fish, usually salvaging an otherwise fishless day.

When the river's water temperature reaches higher levels, fish will seek the cooler, more aerated riffles to wait out the warm spells. When water flows over rocks, it creates turbulence and the water will froth and foam, what paddlers call whitewater when it reaches high enough water levels. Even if the water is at low levels, the subtle rippling and turbulence adds greater levels of oxygen to the water's chem istry and creates a better habitat for fish to rest. These oxygen-rich havens are also cooler because the air has lowered the temperature of the water. When the water reaches above 70 degrees, this is usually where I focus my efforts, as the deeper pools and eddies will tend to be too warm for fish to survive for very long. This riffling water also provides fish with more protection from predation, as the water's broken surface will better hide and distort their shadows, creating a form of camouflage. When fishing these riffles, I tend to switch to more visible and bigger dry flies that will be seen in the broken water but still rest on the water's surface throughout the drift. My all-time favorite riffle pattern is a size 8 Stimulator, which features flashes of orange on an otherwise naturally colored fly and tends to be very effective for a wide range of species.

Obvious eddies behind rocks that are poking out of the water and riffles aren't the only spots where fish may be hiding in the river. Even something as minor as a small boulder on the bottom of the riverbed will create a little eddy for fish to rest in the middle of the current, and a slight depression in the river bottom can create a haven for fish to hide as long as it is big enough for the fish to fit. After targeting the obvious eddies, I'll throw a few casts into the main current as well, especially if the river is not moving quickly, as these smaller, secondary holes where fish can hide might be right in front of you and you'd never know it without throwing a few casts out there. Current deflecting off an object or a protrusion in the bank can also create a seam where fish can rest and wait for passing food. Bubbles on the water's surface or swirling current will tip you off that there is calmer water directly adjacent to the current and you should focus your efforts there.

River bends act very similarly to an eddy, creating pocket water that fish can lie in and wait for passing food to drift by for an easy meal. When water comes around a bend in the river, the momentum of the current pushes the water to the outside bank, causing a pocket of calmer water to accumulate

Professional fly tier Pat Cohen gets the line back on his reel before a 25-pound carp makes another blistering run on the Mohawk River in upstate New York. He hooked up with this fish by targeting slower eddies where carp were resting.

on the inside bend of the river. Fish can use this slack water to hide in the same manner they would hide in an eddy, right along the current seams, waiting for passing forage or baitfish. A river bend also creates a secondary holding position for fish, and usually the biggest fish are hiding in this secondary abode. Where the momentum of the river current drives water into the far bank, the force of the water over time will create a cutbank, or in other words, the water will eventually eat away a trench in the river bank to create a hole where bigger fish can hide and wait for the most substantial meals to arrive. Swinging a large and meaty-looking streamer, with a little flash in the pattern to make the fly stand out better in the darker shade of the cutbank, will usually yield the biggest fish of the day, should a fish be present in the undercut bank at the time of your cast. To properly swing your fly, cast out into the current, upstream of your boat's position, and let the current take control of your fly's speed and direction. The fly will swing out and around, towards the opposite bank and straight into the probable lair of a big fish, therefore completing a realistic presentation of a large baitfish getting caught in the current and flushed into its waiting jaws.

PRO TIPS FOR FISHING WARMWATER RIVERS

One of the best days that I've had on the water when fishing warmwater rivers was also one of the toughest. I was fishing with Kayak Fish PA guide Juan Veruete on the famous Susquehanna and Juniata Rivers, both known far and wide as fisheries that hold behemoth smallmouth bass. The week before I visited, Juan had been telling me about the hundred-plus-fish days he had been experiencing, all high-caliber, trophy-size fish. Then the day before I arrived, a massive cold front had rolled in, bringing near-freezing temps and even snow flurries, causing the water temperature to drop a whole 10 degrees. When the temperature drops that quickly over a short period of time, it makes the bite almost nonexistent. In order to hook up, we had to pull out all the stops and switch to winter fishing tactics, even though it had been full-blown spring only a few days before. Having a guide with vast knowledge of the river's structures and patterns was the only reason we were able to catch fish during my trip.

According to Veruete, knowing where the fish are and the structure they like is the most important part of fishing warmwater rivers. "When I think of a new river, I prepare for the fish first, the target species I'm after," he says. "In most cases for me that's river smallmouth bass, so I'm thinking about the forage that's in that river." Even when fishing new rivers that he's never been to, Veruete tries to get the inside scoop on the structure through copious amounts of research before getting his boat wet. "One of the best things to do is find out what forage is in the water and then try to mimic that," he says. "I'll look on fish commission websites, biology reports of what's in the water, and even on social media looking at fishing reports or to find local anglers, all to find out what the local forage is like and what the fish feed on."

After finding out what the fish are looking to eat, it's a matter of finding the fish. All it takes to find the fish is discovering where they like to hide. Veruete looks on Google Earth or online topography maps of the river and tries to find the best places for fish to hide. "I try to identify the primary theme or structure of the river," he says. "Every river is a little bit different; some rivers are heavily laden with wood, like rivers down south in Alabama. That's a major piece of structure that fish will relate to and orient themselves on." Since all rivers are different, it's not about finding any structure, but the *right* structure. "When I'm fishing the Susquehanna, there are a lot of ledges and that is the major piece of structure that is in that water," he says. "That's something that the fish hold on or use to feed and live in

Kayak fishing guide Juan Veruete releases his favorite species to chase on the fly, a smallmouth bass, in Pennsylvania. Targeting structure allowed him to discover the pattern of the day and hook up.
JUAN VERUETE

those areas better. Once I find out what the major structure is on the river, I try to think about how the fish relate to that."

Veruete has used this technique for rivers across the country and has perfected the tactic to the point of winning tournaments on new pieces of water that he had never fished until the day of the tournament. When it comes to smallmouth bass on his local river, the Susquehanna, he has them down to a precise pattern. "Here on the Susquehanna, if there's a piece of wood in the water, which is rare compared to other structure, it's going to hold fish, but not as good as a piece of submerged ledge rock or ledge system," he says. "That wood is going to hold fish, but it's not going to be a constant producer. So when looking at fishing a new river, I'm trying to figure out what the primary structure is on that river, what the topography is on that river, and try to hone in on some of the key features of the river that I can use to focus in on the fish."

Besides finding out the forage and the primary structure patterns, you still have to know where to fish along the river, which in some cases can run for miles and miles, even across multiple states. Veruete will look at those topographic maps once again and tends to target bends in the river where fish are likely to stack up. "If a river has a lot of bends and switchbacks, you can look on a topographic map and see where the lines are the closest together," he says. "Focus on the sections of river with those steeper areas, because a lot of times, especially in a mountainous area, that means there is a lot of slab rock and big boulder rock that has fallen off the mountain."

Remember, though, that a good angler will always have to adapt to what they see on the water, no matter how good your research is. "There are always things that surprise you when you go someplace, and you kind of just have to go with the flow," Veruete says. "You might get on the water and see that the fish for whatever reason are relating to deep cuts in the gravel in the river and that's something that you couldn't really know looking from afar, so you've got to adjust to some things once you get on the water."

Juan Veruete likes to keep his presentation simple in order to attract a variety of fish, no matter what they're looking to eat. He says matching the shape of the fly to the shape of the bait is most important. JUAN VERUETE

Once you put in on the river, it comes down to checking your research and finding out how accurate all your hard work was. When you get to the structure that you believe is most likely to hold fish, selecting the fly pattern to throw is more about the depth than the color. "You want to get something that looks close to what is in the river, but a bass is not a crappie," Veruete says. "When crappie fishing, if you have a yellow jig and you're not catching, your buddy with a purple jig might still be catching—they really key in on color. With bass, as long as you're in the neighborhood with the right shape, something that looks familiar to them, you'll be good."

Veruete says color is still important, but what matters most is finding the right depth and how you move that bait through the water. Pick a variety of flies that will let you cover the entire water column systematically. Veruete tends to work from the bottom of the water column up to the top in the winter or cold-water months, and then from top to bottom in the water column during the warmer months. "I cover the top of the water column with topwater poppers, the middle of the water column with streamers, and the bottom with something like a crawfish imitation," he says. When in doubt, though, a streamer can be deadly on smallmouth bass because they are so versatile and can be worked at any depth along the water column. "You can work streamers higher, middle, or low, even adding lead weight to the fly to get down to the bottom of the river," Veruete says. "What I do is systematically try to figure out where in the water column I can get bit, on a certain piece of structure, and that'll help me start to put the different pieces of the puzzle together."

While many anglers will stick to the one part of the water column where they first get bit, Veruete suggests experimenting with different depths to make sure you're covering the most productive water. You may be hooking up with a few fish in the center of the water column, but there might be more fish, and more big fish, on the bottom of the water column that you're missing. In order to make sure you're capitalizing on all your research, experiment by testing different parts of the water column as often as you can. "I like to discipline myself, and if I just caught three fish in the center of the water column, I say let me try fishing the bottom and see if I can start catching more or better fish closer to the bottom," he says. "On my mental clock, if I'm fishing something for thirty minutes and nothing's happened, I'm going to start looking for something else to do." Veruete says to make sure you are fishing systematically, working your way down through the water column to the bottom and then working your way back up to the top, to make sure you're in the most productive zone at any given time.

Don't get caught up trying to choose the right fly, but instead focus on finding the fish first and then tweaking and perfecting your choice in presentation until you've figured out the pattern. "I tell my students all the time that on any given day there are going to be numerous different baits that can produce fish for you," Veruete says. "Some days are really tough and there is a slim number of baits that are going to work, but on most days you can catch fish on a lot of baits. The key is locating the fish." Once you've located the fish's primary structure on any given river, the next step is finding out "how they prefer that bait in relation to the structure in the current and what depth they want," he says. When you can find the fish, you can usually catch the fish.

Just like choosing the right fly to put in the right section of the water column, the same goes for choosing the right fly rod, reel, and line setup. "I want to use the gear that's going to put my presentation where I believe the fish are," Veruete says. "I keep it pretty simple if I can. I'll use floating line, because you can usually work a good part of the water column with floating line, but I also always keep an intermediate sinking line with me because I don't fish a lot of deep rivers. The deepest I probably caught fish this year was 8 to 10 feet." Any deeper and you might want to choose a full-sinking line that can get down to the bottom of the water column faster. "Most of the time I'll fish with a 10-pound-test fluorocarbon leader, because I'm fishing for big 4- or 5-pound fish and using weighted flies like a Clouser Minnow." Fishing heavy flies and weighted patterns isn't delicate, so Veruete tends to stay away from tapered leaders altogether, where the leader gets smaller and smaller the closer it gets to the fly. "Because the flies are heavy enough and I'm not trying to lay them out, I use a straight fluorocarbon leader, whatever I can get. There are very few situations where I'm using a tapered leader." You can also use a shorter leader when fishing for warmwater bass, as they are going to be less skittish of your line than a coldwater species like trout or salmon. "When you're fishing for smallmouth, a 5-foot leader is probably going to be enough," says Veruete. "Plus, it makes it a lot easier to have control of your presentation and your cast."

One of the most tricky and sometimes dangerous things about fishing in moving water is anchoring. Without the right system, anchoring in moving water can cause your boat to flip you into the water or drag your kayak under the surface and prevent you from unhooking from the anchor in time. Veruete says a stakeout pole is a much better solution, especially when fishing shallow warmwater rivers, since it can be quickly and easily deployed and pulled up to keep you safe and secure on the water. "A stakeout pole through your scupper or a more advanced system like a Power-Pole Micro Anchor is much better than an anchor," he says. "The anchors I've tried just seem too unwieldy. A lot of times you're trying to swing flies, so having a stakeout pole at the back of your boat where it's not going to get in the way is actually pretty awesome."

Having a system like a Power-Pole Micro Anchor that can be mounted to the back of your kayak will also allow you more room for fishing. When you have an anchor, you have to account for two things: enough line, usually twice the amount of line than the depth you're fishing at, and an anchor trolley system. An anchor trolley system allows you to adjust the contact point of your anchor line to your boat, using pulleys to move the line along your kayak. Using an anchor trolley in

Juan Veruete, a sponsored kayak fly fisherman and fishing guide, sends out a long cast in search of smallmouth bass on his favorite fishery, the Susquehanna River. JUAN VERUETE

a river, for example, you can move the contact point of your anchor line to the stern of the kayak, pointing your boat downstream. If you move the contact point all the way up the front of the boat, you'd be pointing upstream but still anchored in the current. This allows you to keep facing the direction you want to fish. It's also a good idea to keep your anchor trolley system set up so that you're never sideways in the current.

"The more gear that you have attached to your kayak, the more your line will get hung on those attachments," Veruete says. "I clear everything off the bow deck and out of the cockpit of my kayak, including my tools." Any electronics or accessories forward of Veruete's seat are taken off and relocated behind him, so that the deck of his kayak can be as low-profile as possible. This logic even extends down to each nut and bolt placed on the kayak at the factory. "If there is any hardware in the kayak's cockpit that can create a potential catch point for fly line," he says, "a quick way to solve the problem is to take a piece of masking tape and tape over the hardware. It's quick and requires no modification of your kayak hardware." Even the foot pegs in the kayak's cockpit are pushed as far forward as possible—that way line can collect freely at Veruete's feet as he is stripping instead of becoming tangled up.

To make sure rods are out of his way, Veruete attached a RAM fly rod holder to the kayak's hull, behind his seat, with a low-profile Mighty Mount by YakAttack. "I angle the rod straight off the back of the kayak and parallel to the deck, reducing the chance of entanglement on a backcast," he says. "Rods I'm not using remain in their tubes inside the kayak, and the rod that I'm currently fishing with lies on the deck in front of me." Veruete uses an Orvis Safe Passage hip pack, with an optional tippet bar, to store his fly boxes, forceps, line clippers, and other essentials. "It's perfect for the lawnchair-style seat in my Wilderness Systems ATAK 140," he says. "I attach the hip pack to the back of the seat, which keeps my flies and tools out of the way but also in easy reach."

One piece of gear that's harder to keep out of the way, but also completely indispensible to Veruete's style of fly fishing, is his YakAttack Little Stick. "It's a short stakeout pole that you can use in shallow rivers to pin your kayak in place," he says. "I deploy the Little Stick when I'm in shallow slower-moving water through my forward scupper. It finds a crack in the rock and holds the kayak in place." The ability to pin his kayak in place in the river's current makes it easier for Veruete to present his flies exactly how he needs to in order to catch more fish. "It makes it easier to swing flies across the current and target fish without worrying about where my kayak is headed on the river," he says. "If you're a do-it-yourself kind of kayak angler, you can make a short stakeout pole by cutting a wooden rake handle or broom handle to the length of 3 or 3½ feet. That's about the perfect length for this application."

When I was fishing with Juan in the early spring temps, my fingers and toes were just barely registering any feeling, about the same subtlety that the big Susquehanna

River smallmouth bass were using when they hit our presentations. Juan had us focus on anchoring in the eddy of two big rivers, where the Juniata and the Susquehanna combine, allowing the best chance at the most fish. With a swinging presentation we were able to pick off fish, something no one else on the water seemed to be able to do, at least within sight, from smaller fish to true Susquehanna River trophies. Without Juan's knowledge of the right structure and presentations that would work in the warmwater rivers near his home, there is no way I would have been able to hook up that day. I especially would have never caught my personal-best record smallmouth bass, which still stands today.

KAYAK
ANGLER
MUSTANG SURVIVAL

CHAPTER 6

Coldwater

Anglers coming from the world of coldwater fishing are some of the most skilled anglers I've ever fished with, a fact I usually attribute to coldwater species being some of the most finicky, stuck-up, and tough fish around. For fly anglers who have cut their teeth on these hard fish, applying their skills and focus to other species seems to make them one of the top rods on the water every single time they go out.

Anyone who knows me also knows that I am not a coldwater angler. There isn't a species that has frustrated, fooled, and foiled my plans at catching fish more than trout, the king of coldwater species. Coming from a world of saltwater fishing, I simply don't have the patience required to really give coldwater species a shot. I'm used to, and truly most enjoy, spotting a fish, maybe stalking it in super-clear water, presenting a fly within sight, and expertly retrieving and twitching that fly to convince the fish to bite. That retrieve, the special stripping pattern that is required, is what gets me fired up about fishing saltwater. With coldwater fishing, at least the majority of the time, that excitement of stripping your fly in and waiting for a crushing strike is nowhere to be found. Except with streamers, but we'll get to that later.

The majority of coldwater fishing, at least for trout, is presenting a fly without any drag or motion, which is intended to perfectly imitate a motionless bug floating down the river or on the surface of a lake or pond. It's then that an angler's patience is called into duty, as the fly must remain still long

Harry Duchesney holds up and admires his first rainbow trout caught on the fly from a fishing kayak, caught by dead drifting a small Adams dry fly on the water's surface.

enough for a trout to rise up to the fly or let it float past, inspect it, and decide to eat. Whereas in saltwater fishing it's your input in the retrieve that decides whether or not a fish will strike your fly, in coldwater fishing it depends more on your choice of fly pattern combined with the right presentation.

That challenging, but truly rewarding, form of fishing was highlighted when I fished on a tiny pond in the North Woods of Maine with tenkara guide Dan Pierce. Tenkara, which is a form of fly fishing that uses no reel or guides on the fly rod, just a line tied directly to the tip of the rod, provided me with a basic window into the world of trout fishing that forced me to fish dry flies or wet flies, rather than tossing meaty streamers like I've done in the past. Casting those delicate fly patterns, only good for a few casts before you had to take them out of the water and dry them off with bug dust or floatant, and letting the flies float motionless on the surface while you waited for a bite, was a grueling test of my patience. Nine times out of ten I failed and started another cast before a trout had time to strike, as there were more rises within casting range that I couldn't help but cast towards. When I did keep my reptilian brain focused enough to present a fly as still as possible and give the trout enough time to inspect it and decide to strike, I caught the most beautiful brook trout I've ever laid my hands on. It's that beauty that makes coldwater species—the shining gems of the fishing world—worth chasing and getting frustrated over.

Before I first caught a coldwater fish, I always assumed the reason why so many fly anglers chase these species is because of their gorgeous colors. From the deep red of a brook trout's belly and blush pink of a rainbow trout's cheek to the light-colored speckles and spots of a girthy lake trout and multicolored spots of a brown trout, the colors of these fish have captivated and mesmerized anglers, artists, writers, and photographers for hundreds of years, and will continue to do so. That may be the case, but once you hook into one of these fish, you'll also recognize them as voracious fighters, worthy of the chase.

The first time I set the hook on a rainbow trout, even though it was a stocked fish, meaning it was raised at a local state hatchery and dropped into the lake by biologists, it was one of the strongest fish I'd caught at that point in my fishing life. Even after battling with largemouth and smallmouth bass on my local pond, that rainbow trout was the first fish that made me understand the importance of drag on light leaders. Though only about 12 inches long, it sticks with me even now and stands out as a fish that challenged me. I have yet to catch a trout worthy of bragging about, but once I finally convince myself to slow down and focus long enough on keeping my presentation precise and perfect, I'll be well on my way to accomplishing that goal.

Coldwater Rivers

When it comes to fishing for coldwater species in a kayak in moving water, that trickiness is doubled, as presenting flies as realistic and still as possible while you're floating and moving in your plastic boat at the same time requires careful planning. The ability to move your kayak anywhere along a body of water allows more versatility than wading. While some would argue that a drift boat is just as effective as a kayak on moving water, the size of a kayak is perfect for fitting into even the smallest eddies, allowing an angler to rest and fish anywhere in the smallest of places. The size of a fishing kayak also provides an angler with more stealth than a drift boat or wading, as the shadow that a kayak throws off is much smaller and the draft the boat requires to float down the river is much less, meaning the kayak can slide across even the most shallow sections of a body of water. While wading anglers may be able to minimize their shadow, moving through the water, however quietly, will spook fish all around the angler, even downriver, as trout have evolved to detect the slightest clues that a predator is in the river, so moving the rocks and sand while wading can tip off a fish to your presence.

If you're targeting trout that appear to be very skittish, instead of trying to present your fly while you're floating downriver, the best plan of attack is to find a nearby eddy or sandbar that will allow you to stop the boat and present the fly properly and carefully, rather than quickly. Rushing to cast a fly will likely end up messing with your technique and botching the presentation. Often if I spot a fish and try rushing my cast in order to get the fly in the water faster, I end up piling my line or leader on top of the fly or just casting my fly inaccurately, so I always urge anglers of all experience levels to slow down when they're presenting a fly, especially if there is a fish within sight. I know it's hard, but that's going to be your best bet at fooling the fish to bite, rather than messing up your cast and spooking the fish.

In some faster waters it may be difficult to position your boat and fish at the same time. Faster riffles are a great section of the river to fish, as the faster, more aerated water will almost certainly hold fish, especially if the water is warmer, as there will be more oxygen in the turbulent waters. If you can't fish that fast water effectively from your kayak, find a rock or nearby eddy that will allow you to use the boat as a big fly box while you're standing on the obstacle. Make sure not to stand on the same rock or obstacle that the fish are orienting around, however, as your shadow and activity so close by will surely spook them. Instead, try to find one that is a cast's length away. Make sure that casting distance is within your optimal casting range so your presentation is as perfect as it can be to ensure you have the best shot at catching fish.

In order to present your fly correctly in moving water, oftentimes you'll have to add a mend to your cast to either slow down or speed up your drift. Even if you're throwing a fly that requires stripping, like a streamer, instead of a dead drift, mending can be an effective technique for covering more sections of the water column. There are two basic mends that a new fly angler should know: the upstream mend, which will slow down the fly, and the downstream mend, which will speed up the fly.

The basic principle of the upstream mend is to add more line for the current to push by adding an extra loop upstream of where your

With a little practice you can start throwing tight loops to faraway fish, even if you're sitting down in your kayak. Perfecting your cast will help make your presentations more consistent, therefore increasing your chances of hooking up.

line is floating, which will slow down your fly and can also push it deeper in the water column if it's a subsurface fly, like a streamer. As soon as your fly lands in the water, before the current tension grabs hold of the fly line, pick up your line and add the loop to finish the mend after you've completed the cast. Sometimes, though, you want your fly to move a little faster, like when you're trying to fish through an eddy and your fly is moving unnaturally slower than the current. By adding a downstream mend, throwing an extra loop of line downstream from your fly, your presentation will speed up and better match the current in the river.

Practice your mends endlessly, and mend like you mean it. Little mends will often not work as well as a big and more committed mend, which at first will feel awkward and unnatural. With a little practice, though, mending will become second nature and you'll start getting fancier with your mends, even throwing mends mid-cast rather than after you've landed your cast.

Many coldwater anglers tend to favor slower-action rods, even going old-school with fiberglass rods, over the high-speed graphite rods so popular with saltwater anglers. The slower action not only helps protect the softer, often much more delicate leaders used in fishing for trout, but also allows trout to take hold of the fly without feeling the tension of the leader as quickly. This gives the angler more time to set the hook, which is also different on coldwater streams. Instead of the strip-set required for big gamefish, a trout hook set, or trout set, is performed by simply raising the rod tip quickly. Since trout have such soft mouths, the tiny, thin-wire hooks used in trout fly patterns have an easy time sinking into their mouth, requiring only a little pressure from the angler to set the hook. That is why flies no larger than the head of a pin can catch even big fish, though how anglers have the eyesight to tie them onto the end of their leader is beyond me. Many anglers also like that the slower action of a fiberglass rod ensures a slower, more relaxed casting style, which fits the aesthetic of trout fishing on a beautiful river better, like a scene from the popular film *A River Runs Through It*.

PRO TIPS FOR FISHING COLDWATER RIVERS

I admire anglers who spend time fishing for coldwater species, especially if those anglers can catch fish and catch fish consistently. That's the difference between good anglers and the occasionally lucky one: consistency. I love saltwater fishing, and those anglers who are always on fish have my respect, but the ones whose adventures I follow the most are the fly anglers after big trout. That respect, combined with the same aesthetic from *A River Runs Through It* that captured generations of anglers, including me, is the reason why at so many points in my life I've considered heading out west and living among the mountains, rivers, and trout. The pull of big saltwater gamefish, and partly my family, is the only anchor that keeps me living on the East Coast. Still, though, I'll visit as often as I possibly can, because there's no better place to catch giant coldwater species.

One angler who shares who same dichotomy of loving coldwater species but living on the East Coast is Drew Haerer. I've had the privilege of fishing with Haerer, and the guy knows his fish. The first thing he does when looking to fish a new river, like many other anglers, is pull up maps on Google Earth. "Before I fish any body of water, I go to Google Earth and see what I'm up against," says Haerer. "Especially in the kayak, every once in a while you see a river that's full of strainers or gnarly stuff that's just not worth tackling from a kayak, that just kind of changes your approach." He says Google Earth is so good now that anglers can use the imagery to find out not only what is in the river, but also the general type of water you're likely to encounter and what you can expect to find for cover along the banks. "I'll also research local fly shops, outfitters, or any fishing-related information like a hatch chart that I can find for the body of water," says Haerer.

Google Earth, though, is usually just a formality, Haerer says, as an angler who's interested enough in a river system to look it up online is likely to fish it no matter what. "Something's already put a hint in the back of your mind that this river could be fishy," he says. "Rarely am I totaling going out of the blue but I want to try it anyway, but I guess it

The Woolly Bugger is one of the most versatile and effective flies in existence and there are many variations of this popular fly. If you can't find any bugs to match, a general attractor pattern like a Woolly Bugger is a good starting point.

does happen now that I think about it." What Haerer is looking for over everything else is a mix of water, a diversity that will allow him to fish different types of water that he can fish in different ways over the course of the day. "If I can't catch them one way, I know I can catch them doing something else," he says. "Whereas if it looks all the same type of water and I can't get them to bite, I might be out of luck. If the river has riffles and pools and flats and maybe some cutbanks and boulders, and a variety of different types of eddies, I know I can eventually catch them somewhere and develop a pattern in water like that."

After all that research and planning and speaking with different organizations that know about the water, it's time to get on the water. "One of the first things I like to do, especially in rivers, is go find a little riffle and start flipping over rocks," said Hearer. "Most fly fishermen are pretty good at identifying bugs, and I have a science background so I've had some formal training in identifying different aquatic insects and animals." After looking in the water, under rocks, noticing any bugs flying in the air or watching for baitfish, it's time to think about what the fish are doing. "You can walk through tall grass beside the river and see if there is anything darting out of it," says Haerer. "Then, look at the fish—are the fish doing anything, do you see fish rising? Is the water clear enough to see fish moving and actively feeding beneath the surface? I shouldn't just limit that to bugs either, if there are baitfish or something that fish are aggressively feeding on, or a crawfish hatch or something like that."

Those careful observations and input from an angler's surroundings can lead to the best clues for tying on the right fly pattern based on the conditions. "I'll first think about whether to tie on a surface fly, or something subsurface like a nymph or a streamer," says Haerer. Then it's a matter of choosing where to place your first casts. "I always love to find eddy pockets and current seams I can fish," he says. "That little piece of water right between an eddy and a riffle, that's just the perfect spot for fish to feed." Fish will always look for the spot in the river that will allow them to gain the highest number of calories while expending the least amount of calories. "They can sit in that slow water and easily dart over, get a quick bite to eat, and then dart right back, using almost no energy," says Haerer. "Whether it's a low water period, high water, or really any conditions, there's just always fish in those spots; to me those are the most foolproof spots." He also looks for spots with another extra detail that fish might be keying in on, something that will separate that spot from the rest. "Maybe that's a cutbank where they not only have an eddy, but can also go up under that bank," says Haerer. "Something like a little extra cover or some really nice overhanging bushes, or some boulders or logs in the water, or maybe its aquatic vegetation—basically something that makes a seam or riffle stand out more than any other."

Like many trout guys, Haerer prefers rods that are more on the moderate side of the spectrum, rather than the superfast graphite rods used for slinging flies on the flats. "That kind of action just seems to fit my casting style best," he says. "For me, it's just, 'What is going to get you the best result?'" As for rod size, Haerer looks for something that will ensure he has enough power to battle the conditions, but still play smaller fish with plenty of excitement. "I tend to fish on the low side because that's a little more fun for me, so I fish a lot of 3- or 4-weight fly rods," he says. "I totally mix it up, and there's times that I've got a 3- or 4-weight rod, a 4- or 5-weight, and a 5- or 6-weight or something a little bigger if I'm throwing big streamers, all with me at the same time so I can do some different things and not have to keep retying or be forced to do some crazy stuff with my cast just to throw a big fly or something on a rod that's unmatched."

As for leader length, Haerer leans towards stealth. Most of the rivers he fishes in New England are very clear, which means that a longer leader helps prevent spooking fish before he has the chance to present a fly to them. "I like that extra little bit of clear line," he says, "generally in that 10- to 11-foot range with most of my leaders, sometimes a little longer or shorter, and then I generally tie down to a 6X tippet, again because of that clear water. Rarely have I had to go down to a 7X tippet, but on occasion it just seems like they'll snub you if you don't, but I always feel a little more comfortable if I can go to a 5X, simply because if I hook a big fish in a gnarly spot, I'll have a little more confidence in getting him out of there. You just have to listen to what the fish are doing. If they have no problem going with a heavier-diameter leader or tippet, keep doing what you're doing, but if they start snubbing you or something seems funny, try going to a lighter tippet and see what happens."

Constantly being able to change his setup allows Haerer to adapt quickly and stay on the fish. He uses that same mentality when choosing fly lines. "With the different rods, I have different lines on each, and I even have multiple spools that are interchangeable, so I'll carry one that's floating and one that's either a sink tip or fully sinking," he says. Don't be so quick to tie on one line and call it a day, as some fly anglers do. I'm guilty of that myself. I'll spool up a reel with floating line at the start of trout season and forget or just never bother to change it. "There's something about floating line that just makes it more fun to fish, but that doesn't mean it's more productive," says Haerer. "I've learned over the years that there are so many different applications that really work for sinking line but we overlook them because they're a pain to cast or a lot of people aren't as familiar with them—they're just not traditional." Some days the benefits that different styles of line present are too big to ignore. I'll say that I'm going to change my ways, but judging by my track record, I won't make any promises, even though it'd probably catch me more fish.

It takes careful boat positioning to make delicate presentations to spooky coldwater species, especially on smaller rivers like the ones Haerer frequents in New England. He's also not afraid to use his boat as a giant fly box and either fish from shore or a big rock. Just because he's not actually sitting in his kayak when he's making the casts doesn't mean he's not kayak fly fishing. "If I can use the kayak

Harry Duchesney releases his first rainbow trout caught on the fly from a fishing kayak, caught on Cape Cod.

to get me somewhere and then pull up on a rock or a bank and get out to wade and fish, that's usually my preferred method," he says. "I can make little changes that can sometimes be more cumbersome in a kayak."

If Haerer chooses to stay in his kayak while presenting his fly, he tries to stay as far away as his cast and the river conditions will let him. "My goal is to just give the fish plenty of space, especially in smaller rivers," he says. Many anglers overestimate the stealth of kayaks, forgetting that a 12-foot kayak can still cast a big shadow that will seem out of place on a little river. "I think the key is staying back off of fish," Haerer says. "If the fish are just cruising and you're floating over them, just go a ways past them and then kind of circle back from downstream, if you can." Sometimes acting like you're just planning to keep going downriver can make a fish return to its spot faster, for whatever reason, allowing you to make at least a cast or two towards the fish. "Hopefully they don't suspect anything at least," he says.

When he is actively casting to fish, whether they're cruising or sitting in an eddy, Haerer will use his kayak to get into a position that allows him to make the least complicated cast or drift possible. "I prefer to make neutral angle casts, just slightly quartering upriver, to straight across the river, to slightly quartering downriver," he says. "Otherwise your line is floating towards you and directly over the fish or straight downstream of your kayak, which makes it hard to get the right presentation." Those more-neutral casts allow him to make presentations that require less thought and less mending to get the fly to the fish. For example, when there is an eddy in front of you but you're trying to cast farther out into the river, which means the river's currents will affect your cast in different ways at different points along the line, it's very difficult, if not impossible for a new fly angler, to get a good drag-free drift. Instead of battling those tricky currents, the kayak can get the angler in a position to make an easier cast. "In my kayak I can float through that riffle or eddy, anchor in the lower part of the next eddy, and make casts that quarter upriver into the next eddy seam in the middle of the river that is holding fish," Haerer says. "Then you have one less water speed to worry about. Casting across a whole bunch of water velocities like that can make it crazy hard to get the presentation you want. Kayak fly fishing is just about simplifying your presentation and setting up to make simpler, more direct casts."

Much like Haerer's thought process for his fly line and leader choices, fly choice itself must be an ever-changing, ever-evolving process. Instead of tying something on when you first arrive at the river and keeping that same fly at the end of your leader, you can't be afraid to swap flies, especially flies that are drastically different. Even if you're catching a few fish here and there on one pattern, there may be another pattern that will get you many more fish, as long as you're willing to try and to experiment.

Cutting off a certain fly can be hard, though, which is understandable, especially when it's a dry fly. "I think we all love to fish dry flies and surface flies because it's so fun to see the strike, and that's why the rivers are loaded with anglers when there's a hatch," says Haerer. He has also noticed that those same anglers who flood the river during a good hatch cycle are nowhere to be found a few weeks later when the hatches have stopped. The only thing, Haerer says, is that the fish are still feeding, sometimes just as or maybe even more heavily. "There's a struggle to decide, do I want to go nymphing and probably catch more fish today? Or do I want to fish for fewer bites but they're going to be awesome because I'm going to see the strike?" says Haerer. "We have this fascination with surface strikes, and I'm definitely included in that 'we,' but I think that being able to accurately judge the depth at which fish are feeding is really key in rivers."

Finding that correct depth takes time and careful observation. Instead of tying on a dry fly right away, carefully watch where the fish are feeding in the water column and make a guess as to which life cycle of bug they are feeding on. "Sometimes you have to have your flies just an inch from the bottom—you know, just rolling along the bottom," says Haerer. "Other times there's a little bit of a wider window where you can fish the surface or a surface fly and a dropper, or you can fish a variety of different approaches. Finding that sweet spot in the water column and keeping

Take your time getting your kayak ready to fly fish, otherwise you might forget something, like your seat. Keeping the rigging to a minimum on your kayak means there is less chance of snagging your line and messing up a cast.

your fly there is one of the most crucial ways to get bites." That sweet spot and finding the magic mix of depth, current, and fly choice is what brings so many anglers back to the river day after day, and season after season.

Finding that sweet spot is also important when deciding on a rigging style or technique for chasing after these often finicky fish. "Fly fishing can create a bit of clutter on a kayak," Haerer says. "I prefer a large, open deck with few or no accessories and all my gear and additional rods stowed behind the seat." With simplicity in mind, he has relied on a simple clip-style paddle holder for years. "It's such a simple accessory, but it can keep the paddle out of the way while you're fishing and it's still easy to grab when you need to paddle," he says. While he keeps one rod lying on the kayak's deck in between his legs while he's fishing, the rest of the rods are stored behind him. "I generally store one or two behind the seat in rod holders facing straight backwards at approximately a 20-degree angle," he says, "or simply bungee-strapped into my rear tank-well" [also at a relatively low angle]. Since he often needs multiple styles of flies when fishing for trout, Haerer carries multiple fly boxes, in various sizes, just to stay organized. "For example, all my nymphs are in one box on foam so that I can organize and see them easily, while bigger streamers get a more traditional tackle box with large storage compartments," he says.

Haerer stresses again and again that a clean and minimal rigging style when fly fishing will make any angler's life much easier. "I urge people to keep a clean deck and minimize anything that will blow or move around while you are fishing," he says. "Also, if you use a stand-assist bar/stabilizer bar, consider mounting a stripping basket to it, which can work like a charm." He also adds that a really comfortable kayak seat can make those longer days of fishing much more comfortable.

Coldwater Lakes and Ponds

While fly fishing in coldwater fisheries can be challenging in general, I find I prefer to fish moving water. In moving water finding fish is about finding the right mix of water conditions, including current, depth, structure, and obstacles in the water; weather conditions; and, of course, the season. Combining all of those factors into the fish-finding formula, then multiplying that by years of experience on the water, will allow you to make an educated guess as to where the fish are likely to be holding. That kind of predictability is something I can get used to, especially coming from the world of saltwater fly fishing where nothing is static, including the very sand beneath your kayak.

In stillwater fisheries, though, that predictability is thrown right out the window. While there are certain spots on ponds and lakes that fish will consistently relate to, oftentimes an angler is looking for cruising fish. Fish that are constantly on the move in search of a meal, much like saltwater gamefish, are usually much harder to find. Anglers have to use those same clues like current, depth,

Vermont fly-fishing guide Brian Cadoret spots fish for fly tier Pat Cohen at a lake they moved to after failing to hook up on a big musky at a different lake. Scouting a spot before paddling in will increase your stealth factor even further.

structure, obstacles in the water, weather conditions, and the season, but use them as a looser window into the world of the stillwater trout they're chasing.

At least with a kayak your chances are increased because of the added stealth. A wide kayak that will let you stand and fish at the same time will also let you look for cruising fish and/or structure to cast to, giving you a better chance at not spooking every fish you see. If you were fishing a bigger, louder motorboat or wading from shore, much like in a river, your every action is amplified and likely noticed by every trout within earshot. Taking careful paddle strokes and making sure to execute every movement as slowly and as quietly as possible, as if you were fishing on the flats, will give you many more shots at fish than if you were banging and jumping around in your kayak. Even just dropping your rod on the kayak's deck or putting your water bottle into the cup holder too hard may spook fish if they're close by and you don't know it.

Aside from being able to stand and paddle at the same time, always ready to make a cast, a few more-technical paddle strokes can allow you to battle the conditions and position your boat correctly. Many times when you're standing up and paddling at the same time, your boat will start turning to one side, usually the same side that you're paddling on unless there is wind involved, which may not be where you want to go. Instead of constantly swapping sides that you're paddling on, which runs the risk of spooking a fish either by waving your paddle around or accidentally banging against your boat, learn to paddle only on one side. Your paddling will also become more efficient, since your paddle will be in the water more often, not in the air.

Used by canoeists paddling on only one side of the boat, the J-stroke is an effective method for controlling your kayak on one side. Start your forward standing cast the same as you would your normal, seated forward cast, with a strong and efficient catch. Insert your paddle with a rotation from your body, up towards the same spot where your feet would be located if you were seated. Since you're standing, it's a good idea to start with shorter paddle strokes rather than overreaching and throwing off your balance. Keep your paddle shaft as vertical as possible as your blade travels through the water, hopefully completely parallel to your boat. Instead of pulling your paddle blade out of the water and initiating the next stroke, turn your top hand down, so your thumb is pointed towards the water. It helps to hold the very outside edge of the paddle blade that is not in the water, like a canoe angler holding a T-grip. As you turn your thumb downward, your paddle blade's power face should turn out and away from the kayak, thus pushing your stern back into alignment with your forward path.

You can also quickly and efficiently correct your bow's position with a cross draw, which is very effective in winds or light current. As you're paddling in a straight line, you may notice that your bow is starting to stray to the same side as your paddle, which a J-stroke can't correct. Instead, take the paddle blade that is in the water and reach towards the bow. Instead of inserting the blade into the water to initiate a catch on the same side of the boat, cross the blade over your kayak and place it in the water, with the power face facing towards the kayak. Your paddle blade should be parallel to the kayak, with the edges slicing through the water at this point. Initiate the cross draw by pulling the power face of your paddle blade towards the kayak. A more efficient way to initiate the stroke is to actually use your paddle blade as the anchor and drive your hips towards the blade in the water. This will pull your bow back into alignment very quickly, allowing you to pull your blade up and out of the water before it hits your kayak and knocks you off balance.

Return to paddling on the same side that you had been paddling before, or switch sides if the wind is consistently blowing your bow into the side of the boat that you're paddling on. Switching sides will turn the bow of your kayak into the wind with every stroke, and as the wind continues to push on the kayak, you should stay more in a straight line. This is called "tacking into the wind," another paddling technique used by smart canoeists that are paddling on only one side of the boat but still need to control their boat with precision.

PRO TIPS FOR FISHING COLDWATER LAKES AND PONDS

The only time that I've fished with Brian Cadoret was on a warmwater river, fly fishing for giant northern pike on a slow-moving tributary that yielded zero fish but some really good casting practice. While we were on the water, Cadoret mentioned the high-mountain lakes of Vermont that were full of trout, where he spends hours and hours every year in search of big fish on the fly. Those coldwater havens often find him alone on the water, with the entire fishery to himself, which any fly angler knows is a dream come true.

When trying to decide which fishery gets his attention on any given day, Cadoret will gather intel by talking with friends who work at the local fly shops or have been out on the lakes. "I like to fish for wild trout, so I kind of base it on the weather," he says. "If we've just had a good amount of rain, or it's overcast and a little windy, I'll hit those areas that are more known for wild trout." Many of the waters Cadoret fishes, even the ones high up in elevation, are well-stocked with trout. Looking up the local stocking reports will give him a good basis on where to fish and what he'll be fishing for once he gets there. "A lot of times you'll hear that someone's doing really well because they just stocked a lake, so sometimes I will go to those areas if I just want to catch a lot of fish," he says. "I'm putting them back either way."

If Cadoret hasn't received any information from the stocking reports or word of mouth, he'll decide where to fish based on how easy it is to get his boat to the water. More specifically, he'll look for waters that are harder to fish. "Some of the waters are more popular for people kayaking and canoeing, but not necessarily fishing, so I stay away from those," he says. "I'll go to one that's more of a drive, or one that you have to drag your kayak in to get to the water. If it's a little harder to get to, it's almost always worth it, it just takes a little more effort."

After he's dragged his kayak to the water or he's committed and made the long drive to reach water with less people, Cadoret relies on more-common fly patterns to start and then goes from there. "First I target stream lines and where brooks come in and I throw medium-size sculpin patterns and Woolly Buggers, fairly common flies," he says. "Usually I start with a brown, black, or olive, kind of natural patterns, and if I can't get any hits on that, I'll go to more colorful patterns like Zoo Cougars or Madonnas, which are a sculpin pattern with a little bit of yellow in them." As the waters get a little warmer later in the summer, Cadoret will start to look at the hatch patterns and base his fly choice on what the fish are feeding on. "I always carry a

Even if Brian Cadoret can't find a big coldwater fish, there's usually some bass hiding on a neighboring pond or lake so he can feel the pull of a fish. DAN ZINN

second rod with floating line and will carry a dry fly box or a hopper box," he says. "I'll start the day trying to catch a couple on streamers, and then as it gets closer to the evening when you see fish rising, I switch over and will try to match the hatch." Some of Cadoret's favorite dry fly patterns are the Au Sable Wolf, White Wolf, and some common terrestrial flies like Joe's Hopper or Dave's Hopper. "I also like a lot of western-style rubber patterns, like the really big, rubbery bugs that look like golden stones or grasshoppers," he says.

If streamers and dry flies alone aren't gathering strikes from cruising trout, Cadoret will switch to a dropper rig tactic. "I will drop off a small bead-head nymph, like a tiny Copper John or Pheasant Tail Nymph, from the dry fly," he says. "Not all dry flies can handle throwing an extra, but some of the bigger ones like Stimulators or hopper patterns

Fish will orient themselves to structure, like big rocks or weed lines. Make sure to throw a cast on either side of the structure to figure out the pattern for the day.

will work." The dropper rig setup allows you to cover the same water with different types of flies to help figure out the pattern more quickly. "Sometimes when you're seeing the fish rising, it can be a little hard to tell what they're keying in on," says Cadoret. "If it's not obvious, having a second fly below the surface can really increase your chances at hooking fish. A lot of the times when they're looking up, they will see your nymph and they'll grab it, even though they are feeding on the surface." If you start to see fish consistently hooking up on one pattern over the other, you can minimize tangles and switch to that fly alone, or simply keep fishing the dropper rig setup, since it's catching fish. A quick way to set up a dropper rig is to tie on a dry fly pattern with an extra-long tag end, about 15 inches long. That way when you tie on the nymph or secondary fly, you'll have enough extra line to have a foot-long separation between flies, even if you eat up a lot of line when tying the knot.

Another tactic for deciding what fly to tie on is determining the local forage species that will likely be in the water. Cadoret knows the species that he can rely upon to be in the water and bases his bigger streamer patterns on those species in order to catch more big fish. "Almost all of the lakes and ponds that I fish for trout definitely have leeches, minnows, and some small crawfish," he says. "Various Woolly Buggers, sculpins, and if it's a lake with big browns, you can get away with throwing much bigger tandem streamers, like the Drunk and Disorderly and the Sex Dungeon." There are many crazy streamer patterns available that are worthy of experimentation, and the new materials that are constantly being developed are allowing even crazier patterns to be created.

To throw those bigger streamers, though, you need a bigger, stiffer fly rod. "A lot of times you don't need the 8-weight for fighting fish, but if it's windy or you're throwing the big flies around, you can cast so much farther and punch into the wind using an 8-weight," says Cadoret. Normally, his go-to rod is a 6-weight, with a medium action. "I almost always use a clear intermediate sinking line, or a floating line with a sink tip built into it," he says. "This helps get the flies down as you're stripping them in, and I think that can be key. I also carry an extra rod for when I'm fishing dries, like a 4-weight; they store in the kayak really well." When Cadoret is fishing dry flies, the fish are generally smaller, usually 8- to 14-inch fish, so a 4-weight is all he needs to land the fish after fooling them with a dry fly. "When fishing dries, I of course use a floating line," he says. A fairly short leader works while fishing streamer patterns paired with a sinking line or clear intermediate, "no longer than 5 or 6 feet, and maybe 10-pound test," says Cadoret. "These fish, if they're chasing a pretty big streamer, don't seem to be leader shy, and sometimes they can follow pretty close, so I don't like a long leader." For fly fishing with a dry fly, Cadoret will use a full 9-foot tapered leader, down to about 6-pound test. "That's one of the reasons I like to have two rods with me," he says. "You can have one short, stout leader with sinking line for fishing streamers, and for dry flies and terrestrials I almost always have one with a 9-foot tapered leader."

Brian Cadoret searches for signs of fish on a stillwater in the mountains, just after the sun sets. Conditions like this are the perfect time to try throwing a bushy mouse pattern. DAN ZINN

Every once in a while Cadoret will go on a special mission: catching really big fish on a mouse pattern. "A couple times during the year I'll fish mouse patterns at dusk," he says. "I'll fish them on a 6-weight with floating line, usually in the fall or late summer." Usually when the Vermont summer days start feeling crisp in the early evening, Cadoret will switch to a bushy mouse pattern and start searching for that giant. "It's one of those things that you're kind of praying for everything to line up, because if you see fish rising, it's really hard to see the size of them, and throwing a mouse pattern at those smaller fish, it just kind of spooks them," he says. Every once in a while, though, the right fish swims by and a mouse pattern is exactly what it takes to fool that monster into striking. "You're really hoping to find a big trout cruising the shoreline, or maybe downed trees," he says. "Maybe it's a spot that during the day you had a follow from a really big trout while fishing a large sculpin pattern and you saw it go back into a rocky pile on the edge. If you're still on the lake around dusk, slowly paddle up to that area and try to get a couple really good casts with a mouse pattern in that area or other areas that look similar."

When the stars align and you find that perfect mix of cooling temps, the right structure, and a fish that's big enough and aggressive enough to hit a mouse pattern, you have the makings of a great fish fight ahead of you. Cadoret has had a few moments like that, though not nearly as many as he'd like. "One time I had a really big fish attack a hopper and it just missed, but I was blown away by the size of this fish," he says. "I tied on a big mouse pattern, backed off from the area, and went back a little later, but nothing happened." Cadoret kept fishing that mouse pattern for the next week without any success, but the image of that one fish kept him diligent. "One day I was stripping this mouse pattern in, thinking I'm just scaring fish, and this huge brown erupted on it," he says. "It actually came up out of the water, opened its mouth, and came down on the mouse pattern in a surge or whitewater. I ended up landing it; it was a 22-inch brown." Normally a vicious hit like that is reserved for more aggressive warmwater species like largemouth bass, but every once in a while an angler will come across the perfect mix of conditions and aggressiveness in a fish. "This brown came out of the water and attacked it going back down under; it was a pretty crazy take," says Cadoret. "I was unsure if I got a good hook set in it, but I'm really glad I did."

Whether you're after that giant brown or you're searching for an 8-inch rainbow trout on a delicate dry fly, positioning your boat takes the same thought when you're fishing stillwater. Cadoret looks for intersections of structure where he expects trout to be cruising, looking for food. While coldwater species in a river will likely orient themselves on one piece of structure or section of water and stay there, stillwater trout are more likely to be constantly cruising around and looking for food, always on the move. "Normally I'm fishing shorelines, rocky points, around islands, and any time there's a stream entering or maybe exiting," says Cadoret. "I try to put myself in a position where if there's wind, it'll just gently push me along."

As to how far Cadoret likes to position himself from the structure that he's fishing, the general rule he likes to follow is just far enough to get a good cast in and leave plenty of room to have a longer retrieve. "Unless the fish are rising, it's generally not a sight-fishing opportunity, just kind of blind casting to likely areas where the trout will be feeding on minnows, leeches, or whatever they're feeding on," he says. "I'll paddle to those likely areas and kind of just let the wind blow me down the shoreline and hit every few feet, retrieve, cast few feet to the side, retrieve, and repeat." Cadoret will look at depth and features where he thinks trout will be hiding. "You can kind of think that the trout are likely to be cruising from here to there, so maybe those are the cruising paths for that area," he says.

CHAPTER 7

Saltwater

Growing up, I wasn't an angler. I still remember catching my first fish, a pickerel, which I kept calling a "pickle" after mishearing my father, but after that first fish when I was about five years old, I can't recall ever casting a line until I was in high school. Even then, it wasn't until my senior year.

My first car was a 1993 Mazda Protegé, complete with a small spoiler and a thin, barely perceptible stripe running down its side, which was actually a sticker meant to imitate barbed wire. The spoiler was stock, and the crummy window tinting and barbed wire stripe sticker were on there when I bought the car, for the ripe sum of $900. That car, though, allowed me a vehicle to give fishing another chance, with an old fiberglass rod, the thread wraps constantly peeling and even tangling in my line, stolen from my younger brother's swollen collection.

That old spinning rod soon saw a lot of use, and I became addicted to the tug of a fish. It became such an overwhelming thought in my mind that I would routinely skip class every week to go fishing before driving back to school to pick up my younger siblings, grinning wide and smelling like fish, ready to rub it in their faces. Looking back, though, I can't call my fishing at that time anything more than an overzealous hobby. I fished as often as I could and skipping class to fish probably doesn't seem a healthy practice from the outside looking in, but it wasn't a part of my identity, at least not yet.

At first glance it looks like the expansive flats of Cape Cod have no structure that fish will relate to, but after spending just a few hours on the flats, you'll start to see the patterns that will help you catch fish.

This nice Florida snook fell for a topwater presentation and proceeded to wrap itself in the nearest mangroves; careful hands and patience helped to remove the fish from the branches in order to land it. This is the kind of fish saltwater anglers dream of every time they hit the water.

My freshman year of college was a big year. At that tiny school in the middle of a suburb in western Massachusetts, I met the two loves of my life, my future wife and fly fishing. Just a short walk out the back door of my dorm building, through the woods, down a steep hill (read: cliff), and across the road was a trout stream. I cut my teeth those two years on small stocked rainbow trout, fumbling my way into fly fishing, clumsy step by step. When I couldn't fish during the long winter, fly-fishing videos egged me on and kept my stoke level high. The videos that set their hooks deep inside my soul, the ones that kept me lying awake at night in a cold sweat and even threatened my relationship with Jennie (with whom I'm now happily married), were all about fly fishing in saltwater.

The crystal-clear waters of the Florida Keys, sight fishing for giant fish in skinny water, literally made my hands shake with excitement, even though I was all the way up in New England, freezing my butt off all winter. Watching an angler frantically strip in his fly, crouching like a warrior, all the way up to the boat, and then lunging his entire body into a strip-set made my knees weak enough that I had to watch the videos sitting down. That summer both Jennie and I transferred from that school to one in Boston, much closer to home, but also closer to the saltwater flats that my home is known for.

Cape Cod, Massachusetts, where I was born and raised and where my saltwater fly-fishing addiction bloomed, is known as a tourist hub and vacation home location for the rich and famous. It's also home to many year-round residents, which few people seem to realize—but that's a topic for a different book. The waters that surround the peninsula that juts out from the right side of Massachusetts (it's actually an island, since the Cape Cod Canal makes it surrounded by water on all sides, but many would argue that point) are the perfect temperature for striped bass to reside all summer long. After spawning farther south in the waters of Chesapeake Bay, striped bass, or striper, migrate north, following the warming waters all the way up to their northern range in Maine's Bay of Fundy. The majority of these beautiful fish summer in Cape Cod's crystal-clear waters.

Fly anglers have long flocked to the Cape to take advantage of this abundance of fish, and the white sand beaches and miles and miles of flats surrounding the island (seriously, it's an island) can make anglers feel like they're fishing in the Bahamas—until the frigid water, which usually doesn't get higher than the mid-60s, touches their skin. After I started fishing, I wanted to get out in the salt and try my hand at striper fishing. As a teenager and then a broke college kid, the Boston Whaler of my dreams was out of the question, and casting from shore didn't appeal to me. I wanted to get out there, off dry land, to where the fish were schooling to gorge themselves on passing baitfish within casting range of only those fishing from a boat. That's when I first tried kayak fishing.

That first year of fly fishing the flats for striped bass from my new kayak was a test of determination. For months I didn't catch a single fish, until I went out with a guide as part of a magazine assignment. My skills in freshwater fly fishing had been steadily growing, but it took a guide explaining the intricacies of striped bass behavior for the lightbulb to finally go off in my brain and I understood how to catch these fish. Shortly after that fruitful trip, I started catching stripers in skinny water from my kayak, twitching and retrieving my flies while crouched in the ready position, ready to set the hook like in those fly-fishing videos I watched so many times, over and over again. I even managed to get a few fish that actually required those powerful hook sets and have landed a few that I'm proud of. The bug still hasn't been satisfied, though, and all I can do now is lie awake at night thinking of salty dream destinations where I hope a magazine editor will send me, whether I have to fool them into doing it or not.

Landing fish while standing is tricky; instead, kneel or sit down to prevent adding excess force to the leader. This is one of the biggest challenges when you first start kayak fly fishing, but it's very important to practice often.

While the striped bass of my formative kayak fly-fishing years kept me entertained and obsessed to a point of unhealthy levels, and still do to this day, I knew I still needed to test the waters that first seduced me into the world of saltwater fly fishing. After a magazine editor asked if I was interested in flying down to Florida's west coast to fish for tarpon from a kayak, I immediately said yes, cleared my schedule, and packed my bags. For four days I paddled in a little plastic kayak on the hunt for a giant, 100-pound fish that has caused many anglers to give up their normal lives and move down south, fly rod in hand.

The second I got off the plane, my job was to find or source a fly rod, because although plenty of spinning gear was waiting for me at the lodge where I was meeting friends from the industry, I wasn't interested in it. As cool as catching a tarpon from a kayak is, I didn't care about that. I wanted, but really, I *needed* to catch a tarpon on the fly. I needed to feel what it was like to spot a tarpon in the crystal-clear waters of Florida, crouch down as I stripped in my fly, watch the giant silver-sided fish chase down my fly and open its massive mouth, and then lunge with my whole body into a strip-set that would sink the metal hook into the hard mouth of the tarpon and cause it to explode into the air. I needed it for my sanity, even if it led to insanity.

That trip didn't produce even a chance at throwing a fly in front of a tarpon, but it did let me hook into a few fish that were new species for me, including a snook. In fact, I hooked into the same snook twice. On the second afternoon of the trip, almost exactly

This schoolie striped bass fell for a white and yellow Clouser Minnow in the shallow flats of Cape Cod. Small fish like this are perfect for practicing your skills as a kayak fly angler before moving on to bigger targets and faraway destinations.

at high tide, I threw a cast next to a sandy patch amid the grass, right next to a bunch of downed trees sticking out of a mangrove island. I felt the rod double and immediately saw the 30-inch snook explode into the air. That first encounter with the big fish taught me a valuable lesson: Snook are really good at wrapping line and leader in underwater structure, like trees. Within two runs the fish had worked its magic and wrapped my leader around the nearest tree. I lost him. The next day, casting in the exact same spot at the exact same point in the tide cycle, I felt my rod buckle yet again, with a big splash and a flash, showing me it was in fact the same fish as the day before. Two runs later, I felt the line go slack and I lost the fish. Again. While I wasn't able to get to cast to a tarpon, or even see a tarpon, in those four days, I learned a valuable lesson about drag and fighting big fish right next to structure. One day I'll make it back to that mangrove island down on the west coast of Florida. One day, I'll get my redemption against that big snook.

Saltwater Flats

As I've said before in this book, at trade shows all around the country, and to my coworkers and friends that I think might be tired of hearing it, saltwater fly fishing in skinny water with a fly rod is what makes me tick. I've devoted more time, more effort, and more thought into catching big fish in shallow water than I could reasonably calculate, and I've even reserved a spot on my arm for a tattoo of a big striped bass slamming a Clouser Minnow, exploding from the shallow water with so much force, it'll excite every stranger on the street. The kayak is the perfect vessel for sealing the deal with a big fish that would normally get spooked by a wade fisherman or big boat closely passing by. Since the flats most fly anglers fish are so clear, casts upwards of 100 feet long are not unheard of; in fact, they may even be the standard. With a kayak, though, you're much less intrusive on the ecosystem, so your average cast can be half as long as the normal flats angler and still catch as many, if not more, fish since your accuracy will be so much better.

While your stealth factor goes way up when you fish the flats in a kayak, you still have to pay careful attention to how you might affect the fish and water around you. Just because your boat is smaller doesn't mean it can't still spook fish. Always try to avoid paddling over likely holding spots for fish or deep channels that could be a good spot for fish to lie and wait for bait. I always try to fish where my boat is floating towards to make sure my fly gets there before the boat does and ruins my chances. Otherwise, and this is the best bet to make sure your boat doesn't spook fish, I'll anchor up or use a stakeout pole to secure my kayak in one place and let the fish come to me. Fish on the flats are most often on the move, so all you have to do is park next to likely travel lanes and wait for passing fish—just make sure you're ready.

When it comes to picking that boat, you'll want to make sure you get one that makes standing up as easy as standing on shore. The more stable your boat is, the higher up you can stand, sometimes even standing on your kayak's seat or a cooler strapped to the deck. That stability not only makes it easier to spot more fish once you get a higher vantage point, but also makes casting and fighting fish much easier. Stability comes at a price, however, as a wider boat that is more stable is also likely to be slower. While many flats are close to shore, some are offshore, requiring a kayak angler to paddle to them fast, against wind or current, and even flats close to shore can be vast, so having a fast kayak is paramount. My favorite kayak length and width balance is a sit-on-top kayak that is 14 to 16 feet long and 34 inches or less wide. Test out as many different fishing kayaks you can, both sit-on-tops and sit-insides, of varying lengths and widths, until you find the perfect combination that feels zippy when you're paddling but stable enough to fish all day while standing up.

Another key factor that adds to your stealth, or can take it all away, is how loud you are on the water. Dropping your rod on the deck, slamming around tackle boxes, or accidentally banging your paddle against your kayak's hull can spook fish much farther across a flat than an angler can afford. Instead of quickly moving around in your boat, trying to switch from sitting and paddling to standing

Even small schoolie striped bass are feisty and will eagerly take a well-presented Clouser Minnow stripped through the water. These small fish will sharpen your stealth skills so you can start looking for their bigger cousins.

and fishing as fast as possible, try to make the transition as smooth as possible.

The old sniper's saying, "Slow is smooth and smooth is fast," is something kayak anglers can repeat over and over again on the flats to make sure they're careful in their movements. Watch good flats anglers move around their boat when they're looking for fish or have just arrived on the flats, and you'll see a Zen-like calmness to their movements. Nothing sudden, always careful and contemplative, experienced flats anglers can slowly put down their paddle and pick up their rod, strip out some line, get their boat into position to cast, and present their fly, all in time to catch the fish. These careful and smooth movements ensure the fish will not spook, so they will continue to move at the same pace that you first spotted them moving, as they have not yet realized you're there. If the fish spots you and starts moving faster, there's a chance you missed your shot and have to start looking for the next fish. While you can sometimes convince a fish to bite after it moves away quickly, usually by placing a cast where you think it's headed and carefully presenting it, moving around quickly and banging your gear around will only make sure that fish stays spooked and gets out of Dodge.

When deciding where to stake out or anchor my boat, I always try to look for travel lanes where I expect the fish to be and then position myself close enough to cast there, but not so close that I disrupt the steady stream of fish traffic. Fish on the flats love to find different heights in the sand or bottom to travel on—that way they can be ready to sneak up on unsuspecting baitfish that may be passing by. Usually, if there is a channel or even just a small trench running from one side of the flat to the other, you can bet there will be fish moving along that deeper section of the bottom, looking to ambush baitfish that may be swimming across the shallower water above. This same rule applies when looking at the outside edges of the flat, where there is deeper water directly beside the shallow bottom. Fish love to wait along this edge and dart into the skinny water when prey gets too close to the deeper edge, so parking yourself in the shallow water within casting distance of the deeper water will allow you to target the deep water where fish can be hiding, the edge where big fish are expecting to see bait, and the shallow water beside the edge where big fish routinely patrol on the lookout for forage species.

Current also plays a factor when looking for a location to position your boat. Just like trout in a river, saltwater fish will orient themselves in relation to the current in order to gather as many calories as possible while expending as little energy as possible. I've caught fish by letting my fly drift in the current, right over the edge of a flat. Nearly the second my fly fell off into deeper water, there was a striped bass just sitting there with its mouth open. I've even watched striped bass sit in an eddy along a tidal estuary as the water poured out of the system, back into the ocean. The current pushed baitfish through the marsh, right along the seam where the striper was waiting, ready to dart out into the current to feed, just like a rainbow trout waiting to slurp

Stripping guards or medical tape wrapped around your stripping fingers will protect your hands when reeling up on a running fish. Finger protection is paramount when fishing saltwater because the salt will often dry out your hands, which can cause your line to cut through your skin faster.

a big mayfly. When considering the tides and your position, look to fish the downcurrent lies first, but always make sure you're on the lookout for fish that are either crossing the current or moving to a position upcurrent.

When it comes to current on the saltwater flats, there is much debate on when big fish move around most. Some say that big fish only move during strong tide periods, strongest at the new or full moon phases of a moon cycle, while others say that big fish wait till slack tide, the short period between low and high tide when there is little current, to move with the least amount of effort. I've found that both are right, so you shouldn't consider only one or the other but rather both. I prefer tides that are stronger, therefore closer to the full or new moon phases, as there is

A well-stocked fly box will ensure you don't run out of options to give the fish what they want on any given day. Stuff the bulk of your box with general patterns that will work in most conditions, but have a few specific patterns on hand, just in case.

more water moving, which means more bait tends to be in the water and therefore more fish. The biggest fish that my buddies and I have caught, though, was during a period of slack tide, when the current paused and the smaller fish seemed to scatter. A short lull in the action was followed by one of the biggest explosions on the surface of the water I've ever seen, right under my friend's topwater popper. When it comes to tides and trying to decide when to fish, I always tell people to go whenever they have the chance, and not wait for the prime conditions. Always be sure to know what the tide is doing, which way the current is headed and how strong the current will likely be, as that has a direct connection to how you move your fly and where you put your boat. The informed angler will always win over the angler who thinks his way is the only way.

There seems to be a big divide in the saltwater world when it comes to fly choice. While some anglers pain themselves for hours trying to tie up or find the most realistic pattern possible to match the hatch in their local waters, other anglers do just as well following a more impressionistic approach, throwing flies that merely suggest the natural forage rather than try to perfectly imitate it. I fall into the latter crowd, with the thought that time spent trying to perfectly imitate the baitfish present in my local waters is time wasted not actually fishing said waters, especially when those impressionistic patterns have proven to work just as well, if not better. If you side with the former group that likes the perfectly imitated patterns, you're likely to easily find flies online or at the local fly shop to match your fancy. If you haven't made up your mind yet, listen up, because I'm right.

The first thing you have to do before picking a fly out of your box and tying it to the end of your leader is consider what's in the water. What are the fish you're targeting already trying to eat? Once you've identified the local forage, always considering the time of year, as one forage can be present in the early season but nowhere to be found once the water warms up, it then comes to matching the action. I always try to match the size but more specifically the profile of the forage, then the action, with color being the third factor to consider, in that order. When a fish inspects a fly, especially at dawn, dusk, or night when there is less light, or when the water has less clarity, all they're looking for is the right profile. If the profile, as in the shape and size of the fly, as well as the length, is the same as what they're after, they're likely to eat it as long as the color and action aren't so wrong that they get thrown off.

After deciding upon the profile that you need to imitate, think about the action. The action is probably the hardest to identify and replicate, as there are so many fly-tying materials available that an angler could get lost in the fly shop for weeks and still not choose a material to start the first step on their how-to-tie list. Consult fly shop clerks, fly tiers, or local sharpies, anglers who are always on the fish, as well as biology reports on the forage that you're trying to replicate, in order to research what action is most important in your fly. My go-to is any material that will pulse in the water, such as strips of bunny hair or strands of bucktail, as they're not only staples in the saltwater fly-fishing world, but also the most productive on my home waters. Hackle fibers also make great bodies for soft-hackle flies that are perfect for imitating a large swath of baitfish and forage species.

The color, while third on the list of things to consider, is still important. I try to choose colors that represent a handful of different baitfish, usually choosing more natural or subtle tones over garish ones, and have multiple sizes of the same fly to switch between. Flies that are white, tan, and different color combinations like yellow and white or tan and white are good choices to represent many flies. Others that you can experiment with when fishing the flats are flies with a little green, or even pink and orange.

The way you present your fly to the fish that you see swimming right in front of your kayak will largely determine whether or not that fish eats, regardless of whether you picked the right fly. I believe that the wrong fly properly presented will almost always out-fish the right fly presented the wrong way. Many new saltwater fly anglers, myself included, start their learning curve imitating the anglers in online fly-fishing videos, with fast strips and excited retrieves that make some fish follow their flies like an eager puppy. That technique does work for some species in some conditions, but it's not the only play in a kayak fly angler's playbook. Many anglers forget that while an aggressive retrieve can be effective, so too can a dead-drifted fly, a swung fly, or a motionless fly.

Dead-drifting means your fly is floating either within or on top of the water column, without any drag or input from your line. The fly is free to drift as if it were naturally drifting in the current, without a line or angler at the other end. Many times dead baitfish, crabs, shrimp, or other forage will be floating in the current without moving at all, and any nearby fish will see that as an easy meal that they can't pass up.

Swinging your fly uses the tidal current to control the fly's drift and add more action. Casting downcurrent from your kayak or your position, you can let your line arc, or swing like a pendulum, out and away from your position and into the strike zone of a waiting fish. Streamers and patterns with a lot of action do very well on the swing.

Letting your fly sink to the bottom of the flat and not moving it at all, or just barely twitching the fly, can make a passing fish stop, inspect it, and slurp it up before continuing on its way. Many times I've fooled striper that have been either spooked or simply uninterested in a fly on the retrieve by swapping to a shrimp or bushy streamer with a lot of action at rest and simply letting it sit on the white sand without any input from me. This requires maybe the most discipline from a fly angler than any other tactic, as watching a big fish come up to your fly, sometimes within just a few inches, and not trying to twitch or convince the fish to bite means you have to have the patience and control of a Zen master. If it works, though, you can watch the fish slurp your fly and then absolutely explode once you've set the hook, but only after you've given it time to close its mouth, another tricky part.

Whenever you're unsure how to move your fly in the water column, consider how the fish or the forage you've seen are acting and then try to match that. If fish or bait is nowhere to be seen, or the conditions are tougher, like when there is a drop in water temperature or a rising barometer, try different retrieve styles until you start gaining clues that will tell you what the fish want on that day. The bizarre part about fly fishing on the flats is that 90 percent of the time, you don't even cast unless you've already spotted a fish. While there are times when you'll be blind casting, like when presenting your fly in deeper waters or along drop-offs where you expect there to be fish,

Proper sun protection will ensure you can fish year after year without adding sun damage to your skin. Even if the weather forecast is calling for clouds, make sure to dress with some UV protection.

flats fishing offers you a chance to find the fish first and then present your fly to them. While that can be the most frustrating part of fishing the flats, it's also the most exciting.

One thing that always seems to be a factor out on the flats, no matter what the weather forecast says before you head out, is wind. Since there are no trees or obstructions to slow down the wind, very rarely will you find a flat without a little wind, ready to blow your fly line around mid-cast and ruin your presentation. There are many ways to deal with the wind, but as long as you keep your cool and stop yourself from getting frustrated, you can still present your fly as if there is no wind at all.

Whether the wind is blowing right in your face or at your back, casting is relatively the same, though the amount of power you apply to your cast and when changes slightly. When the wind is blowing into you, the tendency is to try to add power to your cast to combat the gusts, but that's actually the opposite of what you want to do. Instead of trying to overpower your forward cast when the wind is blowing directly in your face, add a little extra power to your backcast and apply less force to your forward cast. This uses the wind to add more flex to your rod on the backcast, which then powers your forward cast. The same principle applies when the wind is blowing at your back—you must add power in the direction the wind is blowing. When the wind is blowing your cast forward, add more power on the forward cast and less on the backcast. Your line will have a better chance at unfolding properly, rather than trying to overpower the wind.

The trickiest wind to deal with on the flats is a crosswind, when the wind is blowing from right to left or left to right. This can even cause your fly to hit you in the back if, for example, you're a right-handed caster and the wind is blowing on your right side, causing the phrase "duck and chuck" to originate among anglers who frequently fish in the wind. I've found there are two methods that work best when dealing with a crosswind, both with varying degrees of effectiveness, depending on how much the crosswind is blowing.

If there is a light crosswind, or it doesn't appear to be affecting your cast too much, casting sidearm will cause your line to fly through the air closer to the water, where the wind will have less of an effect on the line. After casting on the flats so long, my cast is now almost always a little sidearm, allowing me to cut through the wind a little better than other casting techniques.

The other technique takes a little practice but it can be an effective method for dealing with a heavy crosswind that is threatening to blow your fly into your body on every cast. Instead of looking forward, with your chest pointing to where you're going to be landing your cast, try turning around and casting while looking behind you. This will cause the line to be blown away from you rather than into your body, allowing you to still present your fly with a degree of control. This takes some practice, but after a while you'll be able to look where you want your fly to land and cast in heavy winds, all while standing with your back to the fish.

Having a faster line speed or faster rod will also limit the amount of push the wind can have on your fly line. When there is a lot of wind to deal with on the flats, no matter what direction it is coming from, minimizing the amount of false casts will ensure your presentation is less affected.

PRO TIPS FOR FISHING INSHORE

Many say that striped bass and redfish act nearly identical, even displaying the same aggressive takes, the same fighting style, and the same devotion in the anglers who fish for them. Just like striper, redfish often cruise the shallow flats all along the coast and the marshes, looking for baitfish, shrimp, and crabs to ambush. Anglers fishing for these species are borderline fanatical, and one angler in particular who stands out is Casey Brunning.

All Brunning does and all he ever wants to do is fish shallow water for redfish in his kayak, fly rod in hand. I can't blame him, after watching more redfish fly-fishing videos than I could ever recall, and I have promised myself to one day make a pilgrimage to the mecca of redfishing, the marshes of Louisiana, and spend a week chasing these copper-colored beauties. I've already spoken with Brunning about getting on the water with him when I eventually get down there, but until I do, I wanted to give him a call and find out just what makes these fish so much fun to catch in skinny water, and more importantly, how to finally catch them.

Even though Brunning's got his spots down pat and rarely needs to research a new area, when he's fishing a tournament he will pull up images on Google Earth and start scouting structure. "You can use that slider tool to see the differences in the times of the year that the images were taken at different tide periods and usually you can see the flats on there," he says. "Then getting out there, that's the biggest part of it." Like me, Brunning focuses most of his time chasing big fish that he can spot in the shallows, sight fishing. "With a fly rod, you're not slinging it all day long—usually you're getting into spots where you're seeing tailing fish" he says. "We do a lot of standing up, looking for tails."

When he's searching for that spot to find tailing fish, Brunning looks for roadside launches that will get him to estuary ponds full of fish quickly, rather than waste too much time paddling. "A lot of the places over the years I've just kind of happened upon," he says. "If we find shallow waters where redfish are holding good, that's usually where we'll start to break out the kayaks or put that down in the book to come back at the right time of the year, when the bulls are actually inshore." That book, Brunning's fish log, is an essential tool that allows him to know where to fish at any time throughout the year, rather than waste time in spots where there are no fish. "Every trip, I try to be real good about logging info, everything I can, like low tide or high tide, the major tide period that we caught fish, water clarity, water temperature, the location, and the wind," he says.

Once he's on a spot that seems to be fishy or he's seeing fish, Brunning will choose one of two flies, a Clouser Minnow or a popper, depending on where fish are holding in the pond. In different conditions redfish will align themselves along the bank, looking down into the water for baitfish, or they'll be off the land more, towards the center of the estuary pond. "If they're tailing just off land, I'll throw a shrimp-looking Clouser Minnow, something with rubber bands on it that'll move around," says Brunning. "If we find that they're floating off the banks and they're sitting a little deeper in the water, that's when we'll use poppers." The right fly also varies with the water clarity, which can vary depending on the season or even the time of day or point in the tide cycle. "In clear water I'm using more of a natural color," he says, "just a light tan or maybe a tan with some maroon in it. If its murkier water, I'll throw Clouser Minnows

High-vis fly line will allow you to track your cast throughout the motions and correct any errors in real time. This will allow you to adapt your presentation to match the behavior of the fish you're targeting.

that are chartreuse and purple; that's kind of my go-to pattern for murkier water." That brighter color in the dirtier water helps fish key in on the fly—that way they're most likely to see it and pick it up. "When they're on the bank, they're usually nose down in the mud, so I want something that's going to get down in front of them fast and I can just sort of sit it there and the hair that's on it is going to do its thing," says Brunning. "When they're out in the middle and floating, that's when the poppers come out. They're quick to find it when you're making a lot of noise with it and they'll chase it for a while"

Some anglers, especially beginners, may struggle spotting fish, especially in murky water like in Louisiana. Even spotting fish in super-clear water against white sand flats can be tricky at first, as you're looking for fish when you should really be looking for movement and shadows. Redfish offer a few telltale signs that make it easier to spot them in shallow, murky water. "What our fish will do, they'll hug the bottom, but for whatever reason, when the sun is shining they'll float up, for maybe ten or fifteen seconds, and you've got to be ready," says Brunning. When you pull into a new estuary pond, don't paddle through it if you think there might be fish in there. Instead, take it slow. "Stake out for a little while or get on the upside of it and drift down with the wind, and just keep an eye out," he says. "I fished a tournament recently where there was probably a hundred fish in one pond but you couldn't see any, so we left. We came back when the sun was out and within minutes a fish would float up on the right and then he'd go down, then a fish would float up on the left and he'd go down. It was chaos for about an hour."

Days like that on the flats are a true treasure and wonder to behold, but you can have more of them if you know how to find fish, even when they're not so obvious at first glance. For those circumstances, Brunning uses a tactic he calls "bulldozing" the water. "Get up on the bank and push them," he says. "You'll start seeing that identifiable redfish wake going away from you; you start pushing them and you know they're there. Once you find that push, just back off and settle down. You'll either see their tails coming up along the bank or start to see them floating up to the top of the water, or you'll start to see that push start moving in front of you."

When you start moving fish or you're just waiting in the center of a pond on your stake-out pole, it's important to be ready the instant you spot a fish. When the fish are only visible for a few seconds, the window you have to make a cast is brief. Instead of waiting until you see a fish to get your rod and line ready, Brunning says you should have it ready before you even start looking for fish. "I'll have my line stripped out where all it takes is one flip from the water to go forward," he says. "If you start with your line at the bow of your boat and you need to whip it six, seven, or eight times to get out in front of the fish, they're going to see you and they're going to get the heck out of there." Even when Brunning takes clients out on his skiff he'll make them strip out as much line as they can cast comfortably and have their line drift behind the

While this fish is small enough to be held with one hand, trophy striped bass can be over 50 inches long. Even small fish like this will influence the water around them and display signs of fish that you can spot and cast towards.

boat. That right amount of line is important to consider. If you have too much line pulled out, more than you can comfortably cast with only one pick-up-and-shoot cast, your accuracy and efficiency is at risk. If you make a bad cast, there's a good chance that you'll spook the fish and miss your opportunity to catch it. You may get another shot at a fish, or even the same fish depending on the day, but there's also a chance you might not.

Having the right rod setup also helps in being ready to make your presentation quickly. Brunning suggests having a rod with a tip fast enough to pick up and cast your line quickly and efficiently, with as few false casts as possible. "I'd probably prefer a 7-weight rod if you're casting a lot, like if you're getting into schools and you're on them all day long," he says. "It's a lot more fun if you can catch them on something lighter." Most of the time, though, Brunning uses a stiff 9-weight with a high-end reel. "I can throw a 7-weight a lot further, but when I get the hook set with the heavier rod, I know it's in there," he says. "I'll take some of the distance out of it using the heavier rod, but I know when things go the right way, I'm going to be able to hold the fish."

The right line can also help you make your cast as quickly as possible, once you spot that fish. "I use floating line and I even use line floatant," says Brunning. "I've never felt like I've spooked a fish when I've got my line floating on top of the water, and I feel like the floating line lets me get it off and out of the water a little better." An 8-foot leader also ensures his presentation doesn't spook the fish. "It's also fluorocarbon, so that'll sink and get the fly down there," he says.

When choosing your other tool for fishing the flats, Brunning says that "a quiet, stable kayak is the best thing you can go for. I can stand on the bow of my kayak and throw the fly rod." A gadget that can help minimize excess moving around in your kayak, thus cutting down on the noise level, which would spook fish, is a paddle holder, one that sits on your waist. "The paddle holder actually holds my fly rod and lets my fly line drift behind me, or holds a push pole or a paddle, whatever you want to move around with," says Brunning. "You can switch between your paddle and your fly rod as quickly as you want to and you don't have to bend down; you just pull one out and stick the other one in and you're good to go." When deciding between push pole or paddle, Brunning will most often choose the paddle. "I've pushed from rocks when I needed to. I can jam it down in the mud or use it as a stakeout pole," he says. "I've always got a stakeout/push pole with me, but the only time it gets used is if I'm going to stake out in the middle of a pond, waiting on something to float."

Brunning says his kayak setup style is all about keeping things clean and simple. "Once I reach my fishing grounds and I'm about to start fly fishing, I remove everything from the Mirage Drive [the pedal system on a Hobie kayak] to the depth finder," he says. "The less things to tangle line on, the better." For fly storage, Brunning wants everything within reach at a moment's notice. "I keep flies in a small watertight box with some dense foam that I cut and glued inside myself," he says. "It usually stays in my side pants pocket or inside a hatch between my legs." Even when it comes to where he stores his paddle, he keeps it as simple as possible. "I have found that a solid paddle holder at waist level has to be one of my favorite game-changers," he says. "While paddling the holder cradles my rod, and while fishing it holds my paddle. It allows me to stand at all times to sight fish and transition from paddling to fishing while always on my feet." When in doubt, Brunning says to minimize everything. "Leave the traditional tackle at home and commit to being a fly fisherman for a day," he says. "Most days I enter the water with nothing but my rod/reel, my small box

A group of anglers prepare their boats to launch at the local boat ramp on Pine Island, Florida, with hopes for giant tarpon just a short paddle away. Setting up your kayak carefully before you launch will maximize the time on the water that you can spend fishing.

of flies, and extra leader material—nothing else at all."

While there's plenty more you could spend money on before fishing the flats, one tool might be the most important for spotting fish: good polarized glass. While some anglers prefer polycarbonate lenses because they're lighter than glass, Brunning says the durability of glass is hard to beat. "Over time my long eyelashes wipe off the coating on the inside of the polycarbonate lenses, but the glass lenses hold up," he says. "They don't scratch, and best of all, you can see in the water." Matching your clothes with the sky will also help you blend in with the sky, aiding in keeping your profile concealed and preventing you from spooking fish. "Wear a light blue shirt, or a gray shirt, or a white shirt," Brunning says, "something that matches the sky and helps you blend in."

Deeper Water

Just because thoughts of sight fishing big fish in skinny water from my kayak consumes my every thought, that doesn't mean you can't catch fish in deeper water with your fly rod inside one of these little plastic boats. I've seen photos of anglers catching giant roosterfish down in Mexico from their kayak, even though there might be 100 feet of ocean below them. From spots that require a short paddle to reach steep drop-offs just offshore to epic mother-ship trips where anglers load up a big powerboat with fishing kayaks and head off into the horizon to be plopped into the middle of the big blue, deeper water can offer anglers a chance at technical, challenging fisheries unlike anything else.

When it comes to finding fish, you have to first do some research. If fish are orienting themselves in deeper water, that means there is some change or character in the sea floor that is making them choose that spot. Whether it be immediate access to shallow water and a steep drop-off or an offshore oil rig creating its own standalone ecosystem, there are likely to be clues that you can draw upon to find your next offshore fishing grounds. Generally, if the fishing is more than a couple miles away, it's tough to get out to the fish, work hard and beat yourself up all day long, and then get back to the shore without getting hurt.

While I've seen anglers get out there under paddle power, if your destination exceeds your experience level or your physical capabilities, you might want to look at a mother ship as your best option. Hitching a ride out to the fishing grounds on a bigger boat with a motor is in no way cheating, it's just being smart.

PRO TIPS FOR DEEPER WATER

Catching fish with a fly rod in deeper water isn't about seeing the fish, but rather finding the right conditions to give yourself the best odds at putting your fly in front of a fish. Conway Bowman has been known to get his fly in front of the fish better than anyone else, which has helped him find his way onto many TV shows in the fly-fishing industry. "I've been the host of a few shows, *The Outfitters, 50 Places to Fly Fish Before You Die,* and *Fly Fishing the World,*" says Bowman. He's also known far and wide as the crazy guy catching mako sharks with a fly rod, fishing off boats, kayaks, and even standup paddleboards. His favorite fishery, though, is the kelp beds out on the West Coast. "Targeting yellowtail is my favorite," Bowman says, "but also Pacific barracuda, yellowtail, white sea bass, calico bass, and Pacific bonita."

When Bowman is deciding where to put in or what area to focus his efforts, rather than looking on Google Maps, he turns to more-detailed contour maps. "Contours create current and current means those spots are more productive," he says. "I also look

Pete McDonald sets the hook on a small snook in Bookelia, Florida, during a paddle through a small estuary system. He tied on a sparse fly to fool this little snook, but was really looking for something bigger.

at the tides. I like to fish big tides, like the new moon or full tide." On certain flood tides, Bowman finds kelp beds that are nearly completely underwater. While no boat can get deep in the flooded kelp beds, a fishing kayak is the perfect tool for getting in there and finding fish among the vegetation. Once there, Bowman says, "You look for bait, like Pacific sardine, Pacific anchovy, and Pacific mackerel." Even in the deeper water, which is still usually only as deep as 20 feet, Bowman can still sight fish by looking for patterns such as working birds or bait schools crashing the surface. Sometimes he can even see fish lazily feeding on the surface. "When you find the food source, you'll find your gamefish," he says. "Then fly choice is all about matching the hatch."

In Florida, fishing with afternoon storms on the horizon is common—just make sure they don't bring lightning with them. Going out into deeper water means you need to be more aware of the weather forecast, since you won't have time to head back in before a storm rolls in.

Late fall in the Northeast means braving cold conditions in the hope of finding a last-chance striped bass that hasn't started migrating south yet. Fishing for striped bass late in the season means going deeper, where blind casting is the norm.

Bowman rarely fishes big flies, because, he says, "it just doesn't look realistic enough." That fly will also be tied very sparsely, as sparsely as possible—"a lightly dressed fly you can see through," he says. "Thick flies look good in the fly shop, but they don't work. You're just trying to give the fish a look. Don't bulk something up; fish aren't stupid." The fly choice is mostly about the outline of the fly, matching the profile to the baitfish. "I'll also match the size of the bait's eye, because a baitfish's eye doesn't move," says Bowman. "That's what the fish key in on."

When throwing his sparse flies, Bowman likes to get them below the surface, so he uses two setups that will let him work different sections of the water column. "One rod is a 9-foot 9-weight, with 350-grain sinking line with a shooting head," he says. "I can fish that very shallow or deep. The second rod, a 10-weight with intermediate line, I'll use that for fish that are lazily feeding on the surface; that line keeps it right below the surface." Both rods that Bowman uses are a medium-fast action, just fast enough to move those heavier lines. "I don't use floating lines; I like to get the flies down there in the water column," he says, and those reels all have 250 yards of 40-pound high-vis Dacron backing. "That high-vis is important to see where the fish is going; it helps to fight the fish," Bowman says. "It helps to keep the right angle on the fish, and a really good drag system is important."

When getting ready to cast, Bowman is careful where he puts his boat, but he says the kayak gives you more leeway than a bigger motorboat would. "If I have fish feeding on the surface, I try to get in front of the fish, and you won't spook them in a kayak," he says. "Still, I position 120 to 200 feet in front of them and let them come to me." A 60-foot cast, 80 feet in front of the fish, will give you enough time to get that fly moving before the fish makes its way to you. "Start stripping immediately," he says. "If fish are below the surface, I'll be blind casting, but if I see them downcurrent, I'll try to swing the fly in front of them." Always be sure to take the conditions into consideration, specifically the wind and current, which will affect the way you present your fly. Tools like a small sea anchor can assist in keeping your boat in the right position. "That's one of the challenges of fly fishing from a kayak—you have to figure out what the fish want and get into the right position using tools like a sea anchor to stay in the right place."

Bowman says preparing to fish from a kayak is a good idea, getting practice in before you get out there to fish. Aside from getting used to using a sea anchor, he says to get used to casting from a seated position. "Be prepared to cast in a sitting position in a small craft, and figure out a line-management system like a stripping basket or stripping net," he says. Once you've figured out the right system for fishing from a kayak and you've become accustomed to casting out of your boat, even from a seated position, it's time to think about fighting the fish. "Make sure to keep your rod tip low, even keeping your rod tip in the water," says Bowman. That lower rod angle will help you get better leverage on the fish, especially when you're sitting down and fighting the fish at the same time. Also, avoid chum buckets. "Never set a chum bucket behind your kayak," Bowman says. "Sharks will come up and check you out."

Index

Note: Page numbers in italics indicate photographs.

About the Author

Ben Duchesney is a freelance content creator, with work appearing in publications such as *Field & Stream*, *American Angler*, *The Fly Fish Journal*, *Kayak Angler*, *Kayak Fish Magazine*, and more. He currently lives and searches for fish near Boston, Massachusetts.